C000059868

# THE GIGANTIC BOOK OF

# WORLD CUP
## Trivia

compiled by Paul Willetts

photography by
Andi Sapey & Paul Willetts

dexter
haven
PUBLISHING

*From Paul Willetts to David and Judy*

*From Andi Sapey to Beryl and Jimmy Sapey*

Published in 2009 by Dexter Haven Ltd
Curtain House
134–146 Curtain Road
London EC2A 3AR

Text and illustrations copyright © 2009 Paul Willetts and Andi Sapey

ISBN 978-1-903660-05-8

A full CIP record for this book is available from the British Library

Cover design Ken Leeder

Typeset in Weiss by Dexter Haven Associates Ltd, London

Printed and bound in the United Arab Emirates

# Contents

# 1930 *Uruguay*

## Group 1

| France 4 Mexico 1 | Argentina 1 France 0 |
| --- | --- |
| Mexico 0 Chile 3 | Chile 1 France 0 |
| Argentina 6 Mexico 3 | Argentina 3 Chile 1 |

|  | P | W | D | L | F | A | Pts |
| --- | --- | --- | --- | --- | --- | --- | --- |
| Argentina | 3 | 3 | 0 | 0 | 10 | 4 | 6 |
| Chile | 3 | 2 | 0 | 1 | 5 | 3 | 4 |
| France | 3 | 1 | 0 | 2 | 4 | 3 | 2 |
| Mexico | 3 | 0 | 0 | 3 | 4 | 13 | 0 |

## Group 2

| Yugoslavia 2 Brazil 1 | Bolivia 0 Yugoslavia 4 |
| --- | --- |
| Brazil 4 Bolivia 0 | |

|  | P | W | D | L | F | A | Pts |
| --- | --- | --- | --- | --- | --- | --- | --- |
| Yugoslavia | 2 | 2 | 0 | 0 | 6 | 1 | 4 |
| Brazil | 2 | 1 | 0 | 1 | 5 | 2 | 2 |
| Bolivia | 2 | 0 | 0 | 2 | 0 | 8 | 0 |

### orld Cup facts

**The youngest starting line-up**

Average age of 21 years, 258 days: Yugoslavia v Brazil, 1930

France was among only four European teams to compete in the 1930 World Cup finals. Two days after beating Mexico in the opening match of the tournament, the French played the brilliant but dirty Argentine team, tipped by many to win the inaugural trophy. Nine minutes from full-time Argentina scored the opening goal. With only six minutes left, their opponents staged a speedy counter-attack which promised an equaliser. Before the French striker had a chance to score, the Brazilian referee inexplicably blew the final whistle, sparking a pitch invasion by Argentine fans. Meanwhile, mounted police galloped onto the pitch and the French players argued with the referee. Eventually conceding that he'd made a mistake, the referee agreed to restart the match. But the remaining three minutes of the game yielded no more goals or controversy.

## Group 3

Romania 3 Peru 1

Peru 0 Uruguay 1

Uruguay 4 Romania 0

| | P | W | D | L | F | A | Pts |
|---|---|---|---|---|---|---|---|
| Uruguay | 2 | 2 | 0 | 0 | 5 | 0 | 4 |
| Romania | 2 | 1 | 0 | 1 | 3 | 5 | 2 |
| Peru | 2 | 0 | 0 | 2 | 1 | 4 | 0 |

## Group 4

USA 3 Belgium 0

Paraguay 0 USA 3

Paraguay 1 Belgium 0

| | P | W | D | L | F | A | Pts |
|---|---|---|---|---|---|---|---|
| USA | 2 | 2 | 0 | 0 | 6 | 0 | 4 |
| Paraguay | 2 | 1 | 0 | 1 | 1 | 3 | 2 |
| Belgium | 2 | 0 | 0 | 2 | 0 | 4 | 0 |

## Semi-finals

Argentina 6 USA 1

Uruguay 6 Yugoslavia 1

## Final

Uruguay 4 Argentina 2

## World Cup facts

**Country with lowest average of goals conceded per match**

0.67   Angola

Accompanied by a fusillade of firecrackers, the Uruguayan team stride onto the pitch, ready to face Argentina in the first World Cup final. Such was the fierce rivalry between the two countries that the visiting team had to be allocated a round-the-clock police guard. Outside the Centenary Stadium, Montevideo, where the final was held, soldiers with fixed bayonets kept watch over the 90,000 crowd as it was funnelled through the turnstiles. With the backing of this fiercely partisan home crowd, Uruguay clinched an exciting 4–2 victory, to become the first holders of the Jules Rimet trophy, named after the President of the French Football Federation. Along with his colleague, Henri Delaunay, Rimet had been responsible for launching the competition, for which the French sculptor Abel Lafleur had—at considerable expense—been commissioned to design the trophy. News of the Uruguayan victory prompted car horns to blare and ships to blow their sirens in Montevideo harbour. In Buenos Aires, Argentine fans reacted to the defeat by storming the Uruguayan consulate.

# 1934 *Italy*

## First round

Italy 7 USA 1
Germany 5 Belgium 2
Spain 3 Brazil 1
Sweden 3 Argentina 2

Czechoslovakia 2 Romania 1
Austria 3 France 2 after extra time
Switzerland 3 Holland 2
Hungary 4 Egypt 2

## Second round

Germany 2 Sweden 1
Italy 1 Spain 1 after extra time
(replay: Italy 1 Spain 0)

Austria 2 Hungary 1
Czechoslovakia 3 Switzerland 2

## Semi-finals

Czechoslovakia 3 Germany 1

Italy 1 Austria 0

## Third place

Germany 3 Austria 2

## Final

Italy 2 Czechoslovakia 1

Vittorio Pozzo (left), manager of the Italian team, discusses tactics with his players just before the beginning of extra time in the final. He and the equally authoritarian Hugo Meisl, manager of the Austrian team, were the leading international coaches of the inter-war era. Experts had predicted an Italy v Austria final, yet the two teams ended up meeting in the semi-finals. Amid the nationalistic atmosphere fostered by Mussolini's regime, Meisl's so-called 'Wunderteam', now past its peak, was eliminated. Italy went on to play the technically impressive Czechoslovakian team, exponents of a fluid, short-passing game. Until twenty minutes from full-time, the scores remained level. Then Czechoslovakia took the lead, only to concede a fortuitous late equaliser, scored by Raimondo Orsi. Retaining their momentum, the Italians scored the winning goal soon after the beginning of extra time, during which Pozzo had trouble making himself heard above the crowd.

# 1938 *France*

## First round

Switzerland 1 Germany 1 after
extra time (replay:
Switzerland 4 Germany 2
Cuba 3 Romania 3 after extra time
replay: Cuba 2 Romania 1)
Italy 2 Norway 1 after extra time

Hungary 6 Dutch East Indies 0
France 3 Belgium 1
Czechoslovakia 3 Holland 0 after
extra time
Brazil 6 Poland 5 after extra time

## Second round

Brazil 1 Czechoslovakia 1 after
extra time (replay:
Brazil 2 Czechoslovakia 1)

Sweden 8 Cuba 0
Hungary 2 Switzerland 0
Italy 3 France 1

## Semi-finals

Italy 2 Brazil 1

Hungary 5 Sweden 1

## Third place

Brazil 4 Sweden 2

## Final

Italy 4 Hungary 2

## World Cup facts

**Longest time on the pitch during finals competitions**
2052 mins: Lothar Matthäus (West Germany/Germany), 1982–98

◀ A desperate Brazilian defender rugby-tackles Fryderyk Scherfke of Poland
as he runs into the penalty area. Although the referee awarded a penalty, it
proved insufficient to prevent Poland from losing 6–5 in this dramatic opening-
round match, played on a muddy pitch in Strasbourg. The unfavourable
conditions led the self-assured Brazilian centre-forward, Leonidas, to take off
his boots during the second-half and throw them at his trainer. By then,
however, he had already scored three goals. At the insistence of the referee,
Leonidas had to put his boots back on. He subsequently scored again, yet his
team was destined to lose to Italy in the semi-finals when he and other
Brazilian stars were rested.

Only fifteen days after the tournament's opening game, the Hungarian team lines up for the final against defending champions Italy, once again managed by the revered Vittorio Pozzo. Countering the technical virtuosity of the Hungarians with their own brand of football, brute force juxtaposed with guile and skill, the Italians secured an emphatic 4–2 victory. While his team celebrated, Pozzo watched, apparently unmoved by the emotion of the occasion.

### Most goals in one match

5 Oleg Salenko (Russia) v Cameroon, 1994
4 Emilio Butragueño (Spain) v Denmark, 1986
4 Eusebio (Portugal) v North Korea, 1966
4 Just Fontaine (France) v West Germany, 1958
4 Sándor Kocsis (Hungary) v West Germany, 1954
4 Ademir (Brazil) v Sweden, 1950
4 Juan Schiaffino (Uruguay) v Bolivia, 1950
4 Ernst Willimowski (Poland) v Brazil, 1938
4 Gustav Wetterström (Sweden) v Cuba, 1938

**Most common result in World Cup matches**
1–0

### Most appearances in finals tournaments

25 Lothar Matthäus (West Germany/Germany)
23 Paolo Maldini (Italy)
21 Diego Maradona (Argentina)
21 Wladislav Zmuda (Poland)
21 Uwe Seeler (West Germany)
20 Grzegorz Lato (Poland)
20 Cafu (Brazil)
19 Berti Vogts (West Germany)
19 Karl-Heinz Rummenigge (West Germany)
19 Wolfgang Overath (West Germany)
19 Ronaldo (Brazil)

**Only one-armed man to have played in the finals**
Héctor Castro (Uruguay) who had, aged 13, lost his right forearm while using an electric saw. Nicknamed 'El manco' (which means, unsurprisingly, 'one-armed') his goal in the 1930 final helped his country win the first ever World Cup.

Italian forward Gino Colaussi beats the Hungarian goalkeeper in his team's comprehensive victory in the final. But the outbreak of the Second World War just under fifteen months later meant that the Italians would have to wait twelve years before defending their trophy, by which time Pozzo's long and successful reign as manager had ended.

# 1950 *Brazil*

## Group 1

| | | Brazil 4 Mexico 0 | | | | Brazil 2 Switzerland 2 | | |
| Yugoslavia 3 Switzerland 0 | | | | | | Yugoslavia 4 Mexico 1 | | |
| Brazil 2 Yugoslavia 0 | | | | | | Switzerland 2 Mexico 1 | | |

| | P | W | D | L | F | A | Pts |
|---|---|---|---|---|---|---|---|
| Brazil | 3 | 2 | 1 | 0 | 8 | 2 | 5 |
| Yugoslavia | 3 | 2 | 0 | 1 | 7 | 3 | 4 |
| Switzerland | 3 | 1 | 1 | 1 | 4 | 6 | 3 |
| Mexico | 3 | 0 | 0 | 3 | 2 | 10 | 0 |

## Group 2

Spain 3 USA 1                     England 2 Chile 0
USA 1 England 0                   Spain 2 Chile 0
Spain 1 England 0                 Chile 5 USA 2

| | P | W | D | L | F | A | Pts |
|---|---|---|---|---|---|---|---|
| Spain | 3 | 3 | 0 | 0 | 6 | 1 | 6 |
| England | 3 | 1 | 0 | 2 | 2 | 2 | 2 |
| Chile | 3 | 1 | 0 | 2 | 5 | 6 | 2 |
| USA | 3 | 1 | 0 | 2 | 4 | 8 | 2 |

## Group 3

Sweden 3 Italy 2                  Sweden 2 Paraguay 2
Italy 2 Paraguay 0

| | P | W | D | L | F | A | Pts |
|---|---|---|---|---|---|---|---|
| Sweden | 2 | 1 | 1 | 0 | 5 | 4 | 3 |
| Italy | 2 | 1 | 0 | 1 | 4 | 3 | 2 |
| Paraguay | 2 | 0 | 1 | 1 | 2 | 4 | 1 |

◢ The diminutive twenty-year-old, 'Nacka' Skoglund, pauses for a breather during Sweden's 7–1 final group game defeat by Brazil. His emergence as a classy international footballer had been both rapid and perfectly timed. Until he had signed for AIK Stockholm, just before the beginning of the tournament, he had played in the Swedish third division. His new club provided a perfect platform for the skills that would make him a key member of the national team, coached by George Raynor, an Englishman whose previous experience consisted of a spell as a reserve-team club manager. The innovative Raynor nonetheless succeeded in making Sweden a major force in the international game.

Uruguay 8 Bolivia 0

|  | P | W | D | L | F | A | Pts |
|--------|---|---|---|---|----|----|-----|
| Uruguay | 1 | 1 | 0 | 0 | 8 | 0 | 2 |
| Bolivia | 1 | 0 | 0 | 1 | 0 | 8 | 0 |

**Final group**

Uruguay 2 Spain 2          Brazil 7 Sweden 1
Uruguay 3 Sweden 2         Brazil 6 Spain 1
Sweden 3 Spain 1           Uruguay 2 Brazil 1

|  | P | W | D | L | F | A | Pts |
|--------|---|---|---|---|----|----|-----|
| Uruguay | 3 | 2 | 1 | 0 | 7 | 5 | 5 |
| Brazil | 3 | 2 | 0 | 1 | 14 | 4 | 4 |
| Sweden | 3 | 1 | 0 | 2 | 6 | 11 | 2 |
| Spain | 3 | 0 | 1 | 2 | 4 | 11 | 1 |

**Winner**

Uruguay

**World Cup facts**

**Most matches played in finals tournaments**
92 Germany/West Germany
92 Brazil

**World Cup facts**

**Most cards shown in one match**
16 Germany v Cameroon, 2002

In front of a World Cup record-breaking crowd of 199,854, many of whom had forced their way through the gates of the Maracanã Stadium, Alcides Ghiggia of Uruguay strikes the winning goal in the tournament's climactic match. For the only time in the history of the competition, the concluding knockout rounds were replaced by a single mini-league, which Uruguay topped, courtesy of this victory against Brazil. Regarded as overwhelming favourites, the home nation possessed an impressive forward line that blended artistry and athleticism. But they were overcome by the less talented, more resilient Uruguayan line-up which had already beaten them once that year.

# 1954 *Switzerland*

## Group 1

Yugoslavia 1 France 0
France 3 Mexico 2

Brazil 5 Mexico 0
Brazil 1 Yugoslavia 1 after extra time

| | P | W | D | L | F | A | Pts |
|---|---|---|---|---|---|---|---|
| Brazil | 2 | 1 | 1 | 0 | 6 | 1 | 3 |
| Yugoslavia | 2 | 1 | 1 | 0 | 2 | 1 | 3 |
| France | 2 | 1 | 0 | 1 | 3 | 3 | 2 |
| Mexico | 2 | 0 | 0 | 2 | 2 | 8 | 0 |

## Group 2

Hungary 9 South Korea 0
Hungary 8 West Germany 3
play-off: West Germany 7 Turkey 2

West Germany 4 Turkey 1
Turkey 7 South Korea 0

| | P | W | D | L | F | A | Pts |
|---|---|---|---|---|---|---|---|
| Hungary | 2 | 2 | 0 | 0 | 17 | 3 | 4 |
| West Germany | 3 | 2 | 0 | 1 | 14 | 11 | 4 |
| Turkey | 3 | 1 | 0 | 2 | 10 | 11 | 2 |
| South Korea | 2 | 0 | 0 | 2 | 0 | 16 | 0 |

## Group 3

Austria 1 Scotland 0
Austria 5 Czechoslovakia 0

Uruguay 2 Czechoslovakia 0
Uruguay 7 Scotland 0

| | P | W | D | L | F | A | Pts |
|---|---|---|---|---|---|---|---|
| Uruguay | 2 | 2 | 0 | 0 | 9 | 0 | 4 |
| Austria | 2 | 2 | 0 | 0 | 6 | 0 | 4 |
| Czechoslovakia | 2 | 0 | 0 | 2 | 0 | 7 | 0 |
| Scotland | 2 | 0 | 0 | 2 | 0 | 8 | 0 |

◼ Gyula Mandi, coach of the Hungarian team, issues instructions to his side's centre-forward Nandor Hidegkuti during the quarter-final against Brazil—the so-called 'Battle of Berne'. Only the superb refereeing of Arthur Ellis prevented the game from degenerating into a brawl. After the final whistle, the Brazilian team burst into the opposition dressing-room. According to an account published in the Italian newspaper *Corriere della Sera*, Ferenc Puskas, the Hungarian midfielder, who hadn't played due to an earlier injury, struck one of the Brazilian players in the face with a bottle, causing a wound 8cm long.

## Group 4

| | | | | | | | |
|---|---|---|---|---|---|---|---|
| England 4 Belgium 4 after extra time | | | | England 2 Switzerland 0 | | | |
| Switzerland 2 Italy 1 | | | | Italy 4 Belgium 1 | | | |
| play-off: Switzerland 4 Italy 1 | | | | | | | |

| | P | W | D | L | F | A | Pts |
|---|---|---|---|---|---|---|---|
| England | 2 | 1 | 1 | 0 | 6 | 4 | 3 |
| Switzerland | 3 | 2 | 0 | 1 | 6 | 4 | 4 |
| Italy | 3 | 1 | 0 | 2 | 6 | 7 | 2 |
| Belgium | 2 | 0 | 1 | 1 | 5 | 8 | 1 |

## Quarter-finals

West Germany 2 Yugoslavia 0          Hungary 4 Brazil 2
Austria 7 Switzerland 5              Uruguay 4 England 2

## Semi-finals

West Germany 6 Austria 1
Hungary 4 Uruguay 2 after extra time

## Third place

Austria 3 Uruguay 1

## Final

West Germany 3 Hungary 2

### World Cup facts

**Most goals by a team in one competition**
27 Hungary, 1954

The West German team celebrates Helmut Rahn's winning goal in the final. Dubbed 'the Miracle of Berne', the game saw the unfancied Germans defeat Hungary—'the Mighty Magyars'—in one of the biggest upsets in World Cup history. During the run-up to the tournament, the Hungarians had won the Olympic title, playing a new brand of football that blended power and precision. Captained by Ferenc Puskas, a dumpy little man whose physique belied his supreme skill, they were widely accepted as champions-in-waiting. During his side's 8–3 defeat of West Germany in the opening round of matches, he sustained an injury when he was heavily tackled by the hulking German centre-half, Werner Liebrich. This may well have been the moment that denied his team the trophy. Even though he played in the final, he wasn't fit enough to exert his usual dynamic influence.

23

# 1958 *Sweden*

## Group 1

| | | | | | | | |
|---|---|---|---|---|---|---|---|
| West Germany 3 Argentina 1 | | | | Northern Ireland 1 Czechoslovakia 0 | | | |
| West Germany 2 Czechoslovakia 2 | | | | Argentina 3 Northern Ireland 1 | | | |
| West Germany 2 Northern Ireland 2 | | | | Czechoslovakia 6 Argentina 1 | | | |
| play-off: Northern Ireland 2 Czechoslovakia 1 after extra time | | | | | | | |

| | P | W | D | L | F | A | Pts |
|---|---|---|---|---|---|---|---|
| West Germany | 3 | 1 | 2 | 0 | 7 | 5 | 4 |
| Northern Ireland | 4 | 2 | 1 | 1 | 6 | 6 | 5 |
| Czechoslovakia | 4 | 1 | 1 | 2 | 9 | 6 | 3 |
| Argentina | 3 | 1 | 0 | 2 | 5 | 10 | 2 |

## Group 2

| | | | | | | | |
|---|---|---|---|---|---|---|---|
| France 7 Paraguay 3 | | | | Yugoslavia 1 Scotland 1 | | | |
| France 2 Yugoslavia 3 | | | | Paraguay 3 Scotland 2 | | | |
| France 2 Scotland 1 | | | | Yugoslavia 3 Paraguay 3 | | | |

| | P | W | D | L | F | A | Pts |
|---|---|---|---|---|---|---|---|
| France | 3 | 2 | 0 | 1 | 11 | 7 | 4 |
| Yugoslavia | 3 | 1 | 2 | 0 | 7 | 6 | 4 |
| Paraguay | 3 | 1 | 1 | 1 | 9 | 12 | 3 |
| Scotland | 3 | 0 | 1 | 2 | 4 | 6 | 1 |

Northern Ireland goalkeeper Harry Gregg attempts to prevent Uwe Seeler's equalising goal in the opening-round 2–2 draw with West Germany. Gregg was part of a talented group of players that included Danny Blanchflower and Billy Bingham. Under the imaginative leadership of Peter Doherty, their team had exceeded expectations by qualifying for the tournament at the expense of Italy. But their participation in the finals was briefly endangered due to a religious campaign waged against them playing on Sundays—a necessity during a World Cup campaign. Despite their underdog status, they fought their way through to the quarter-finals, where they were overwhelmed by the French team, which featured Just Fontaine and Raymond Kopa, two of the undisputed stars of the competition.

## Group 3

Sweden 3 Mexico 0
Wales 1 Mexico 1
Sweden 0 Wales 0
play-off: Wales 2 Hungary 1

Hungary 1 Wales 1
Sweden 2 Hungary 1
Hungary 4 Mexico 0

|         | P | W | D | L | F | A | Pts |
|---------|---|---|---|---|---|---|-----|
| Sweden  | 3 | 2 | 1 | 0 | 5 | 1 | 5   |
| Wales   | 4 | 1 | 3 | 0 | 4 | 3 | 5   |
| Hungary | 4 | 1 | 1 | 2 | 7 | 5 | 3   |
| Mexico  | 3 | 0 | 1 | 2 | 1 | 8 | 1   |

## Group 4

England 2 Soviet Union 2
England 0 Brazil 0
Brazil 2 Soviet Union 0
play-off: Soviet Union 1 England 0

Brazil 3 Austria 0
Soviet Union 2 Austria 0
England 2 Austria 2

|              | P | W | D | L | F | A | Pts |
|--------------|---|---|---|---|---|---|-----|
| Brazil       | 3 | 2 | 1 | 0 | 5 | 0 | 5   |
| Soviet Union | 4 | 2 | 1 | 1 | 5 | 4 | 5   |
| England      | 4 | 0 | 3 | 1 | 4 | 5 | 3   |
| Austria      | 3 | 0 | 1 | 2 | 2 | 7 | 1   |

### World Cup facts

**Most hat-tricks in finals tournaments**

2  Sándor Kocsis (Hungary)
2  Just Fontaine (France)
2  Gerd Müller (West Germany)
2  Gabriel Batistuta (Argentina)

### World Cup facts

**Most matches played without a win in finals tournaments**

6  Bolivia
6  El Salvador

◀ Swedish goalkeeper, Karl Svensson, is challenged by 17-year-old Edison Arantes do Nascimento—better known as 'Pelé'—in the 1958 final in Stockholm, where Brazil won 5–2. The tournament was distinguished by the emergence of both Pelé and the now commonplace 4–4–2 formation. Already rated as one of the best players produced by his country, Pelé was the protegé of the former Brazilian international forward de Brito. So precocious was Pelé that he'd been playing for Brazil since the previous year. But he was injured when the tournament began. He had to wait until his country's last group match—a one-sided victory against the Soviet Union—before making his debut in the World Cup finals.

## Quarter-finals

| | |
|---|---|
| France 4 Northern Ireland 0 | Sweden 2 Soviet Union 0 |
| West Germany 1 Yugoslavia 0 | Brazil 1 Wales 0 |

## Semi-finals

| | |
|---|---|
| Brazil 5 France 2 | Sweden 3 West Germany 1 |

## Third place

France 6 West Germany 3

## Final

Brazil 5 Sweden 2

### World Cup facts

**Only tournament when the champions refused to defend their title**

1934 Still peeved by the lack of interest from Europe in the inaugural competition, held in Montevideo, the Uruguayan team didn't defend the trophy they had won four years earlier.

### Strange but true

The match between Brazil and England in the 1962 finals was interrupted by a dog which ran onto the pitch.

◀ Perching on the shoulders of a jubilant team-mate, Pelé celebrates his country's victory in the World Cup final. Ten minutes after half-time, he'd scored the goal that had broken Sweden's resistance. Standing in the penalty area, he'd controlled the ball on his thigh, then clipped it over his head, spun round and volleyed it past the goalkeeper. From that moment onwards, the Brazilians dominated the game, their supporters chanting 'Samba! Samba!'

# 1962 *Chile*

## Group 1

| Uruguay 2 Colombia 1 | Soviet Union 2 Yugoslavia 0 |
|---|---|
| Yugoslavia 3 Uruguay 1 | Soviet Union 4 Colombia 4 |
| Soviet Union 2 Uruguay 1 | Yugoslavia 5 Colombia 0 |

|  | P | W | D | L | F | A | Pts |
|---|---|---|---|---|---|---|---|
| Soviet Union | 3 | 2 | 1 | 0 | 8 | 5 | 5 |
| Yugoslavia | 3 | 2 | 0 | 1 | 8 | 3 | 4 |
| Uruguay | 3 | 1 | 0 | 2 | 4 | 6 | 2 |
| Colombia | 3 | 0 | 1 | 2 | 5 | 11 | 1 |

## Group 2

| Chile 3 Switzerland 1 | West Germany 0 Italy 0 |
|---|---|
| West Germany 2 Switzerland 1 | Chile 2 Italy 0 |
| Chile 0 West Germany 2 | Italy 3 Switzerland 0 |

|  | P | W | D | L | F | A | Pts |
|---|---|---|---|---|---|---|---|
| West Germany | 3 | 2 | 1 | 0 | 4 | 1 | 5 |
| Chile | 3 | 2 | 0 | 1 | 5 | 3 | 4 |
| Italy | 3 | 1 | 1 | 1 | 3 | 2 | 3 |
| Switzerland | 3 | 0 | 0 | 3 | 2 | 8 | 0 |

### orld Cup facts

**Most matches played by a country without scoring a goal**

3   Canada
3   China
3   Greece
3   Trinidad and Tobago
3   Zaire

A crowd of angry players forms during Chile's opening-round victory over Italy, which would become known as 'the Battle of Santiago'. Hostility between the two sides had developed as a result of two disparaging articles about the Chilean team written by Italian journalists. The situation wasn't helped by the presence of Italian scouts spying on the South Americans' training camp. These factors contributed to a match of such brutality that one player suffered a broken nose and two others were sent off.

## Group 3

Brazil 2 Mexico 0
Brazil 0 Czechoslovakia 0
Brazil 2 Spain 1

Czechoslovakia 1 Spain 0
Spain 1 Mexico 0
Mexico 3 Czechoslovakia 1

|  | P | W | D | L | F | A | Pts |
|---|---|---|---|---|---|---|---|
| Brazil | 3 | 2 | 1 | 0 | 4 | 1 | 5 |
| Czechoslovakia | 3 | 1 | 1 | 1 | 2 | 3 | 3 |
| Mexico | 3 | 1 | 0 | 2 | 3 | 4 | 2 |
| Spain | 3 | 1 | 0 | 2 | 2 | 3 | 2 |

## Group 4

Argentina 1 Bulgaria 0
Argentina 1 England 3
Argentina 0 Hungary 0

Hungary 2 England 1
Hungary 6 Bulgaria 1
England 0 Bulgaria 0

|  | P | W | D | L | F | A | Pts |
|---|---|---|---|---|---|---|---|
| Hungary | 3 | 2 | 1 | 0 | 8 | 2 | 5 |
| England | 3 | 1 | 1 | 1 | 4 | 3 | 3 |
| Argentina | 3 | 1 | 1 | 1 | 2 | 3 | 3 |
| Bulgaria | 3 | 0 | 1 | 2 | 1 | 7 | 1 |

## Quarter-finals

Yugoslavia 1 West Germany 0
Chile 2 Soviet Union 1

Brazil 3 England 1
Czechoslovakia 1 Hungary 0

## Semi-finals

Czechoslovakia 3 Yugoslavia 1

Brazil 4 Chile 2

## Third place

Chile 1 Yugoslavia 0

## Final

Brazil 3 Czechoslovakia 1

Russian goalkeeper Lev Yashin pulls off a spectacular save in the Soviet Union's 2–0 quarter-final defeat by Sweden. Only the previous November, the Russians had signalled their status as dark-horses for the tournament by beating favourites Uruguay during a triumphant tour of South America. But this optimism was undermined by Yashin's inconsistency, embarrassing errors punctuating his accustomed brilliance. After his erratic performance in the group game against Colombia, *L'Équipe*—the French sports newspaper—declared that this match 'marked an historic date, the end of the greatest modern goalkeeper, if not of all time: Lev Yashin'.

FULL REPORTS IN THE
SUNDAY EXPRESS
FULL REPORTS IN THE
SUNDAY EXPRESS
Mars
Mars

# 1966 *England*

## Group 1

England 0 Uruguay 0
Uruguay 2 France 1
Uruguay 0 Mexico 0

France 1 Mexico 1
England 2 Mexico 0
England 2 France 0

|         | P | W | D | L | F | A | Pts |
|---------|---|---|---|---|---|---|-----|
| England | 3 | 2 | 1 | 0 | 4 | 0 | 5   |
| Uruguay | 3 | 1 | 2 | 0 | 2 | 1 | 4   |
| Mexico  | 3 | 0 | 2 | 1 | 1 | 3 | 2   |
| France  | 3 | 0 | 1 | 2 | 2 | 5 | 1   |

## Group 2

West Germany 5 Switzerland 0
Spain 2 Switzerland 1
Argentina 0 West Germany 0

Argentina 2 Spain 1
Argentina 2 Switzerland 0
West Germany 2 Spain 1

|              | P | W | D | L | F | A | Pts |
|--------------|---|---|---|---|---|---|-----|
| West Germany | 3 | 2 | 1 | 0 | 7 | 1 | 5   |
| Argentina    | 3 | 2 | 1 | 0 | 4 | 1 | 5   |
| Spain        | 3 | 1 | 0 | 2 | 4 | 5 | 2   |
| Switzerland  | 3 | 0 | 0 | 3 | 1 | 9 | 0   |

## orld Cup facts

Total number of spectators who have attended matches at the finals
30,930,100

The crowd at Ayresome Park, Middlesbrough watch outsiders North Korea, hamstrung by over-cautious tactics, succumb to a 3–0 defeat in their opening game against the Soviet Union. Little was known about them before the tournament, but they soon established a surprising rapport with the Teesside public, many of whom started referring to the North Koreans as 'us'. Forced into a more adventurous style of play, the team came from behind to obtain a 1–1 draw with Chile. In their final match of the opening stages, the North Koreans sprang one of the greatest surprises in World Cup history, using their pace to defeat Italy.

| | | | | | | |
|---|---|---|---|---|---|---|
| Brazil 2 Bulgaria 0 | | | | Portugal 3 Hungary 1 | | |
| Hungary 3 Brazil 1 | | | | Portugal 3 Bulgaria 0 | | |
| Brazil 1 Portugal 3 | | | | Hungary 3 Bulgaria 1 | | |

| | P | W | D | L | F | A | Pts |
|---|---|---|---|---|---|---|---|
| Portugal | 3 | 3 | 0 | 0 | 9 | 2 | 6 |
| Hungary | 3 | 2 | 0 | 1 | 7 | 5 | 4 |
| Brazil | 3 | 1 | 0 | 2 | 4 | 6 | 2 |
| Bulgaria | 3 | 0 | 0 | 3 | 1 | 8 | 0 |

## Group 4

| | | | | | | |
|---|---|---|---|---|---|---|
| Soviet Union 3 North Korea 0 | | | | Italy 2 Chile 0 | | |
| Chile 1 North Korea 1 | | | | Soviet Union 1 Italy 0 | | |
| North Korea 1 Italy 0 | | | | Soviet Union 2 Chile 1 | | |

| | P | W | D | L | F | A | Pts |
|---|---|---|---|---|---|---|---|
| Soviet Union | 3 | 3 | 0 | 0 | 6 | 1 | 6 |
| North Korea | 3 | 1 | 1 | 1 | 2 | 4 | 3 |
| Italy | 3 | 1 | 0 | 2 | 2 | 2 | 2 |
| Chile | 3 | 0 | 1 | 2 | 2 | 5 | 1 |

## World Cup facts

**Times the original World Cup trophy was stolen**

Twice. In the run-up to the 1966 tournament, the Jules Rimet trophy was stolen from the Central Hall in Westminster, where it was being displayed. It was later discovered by David Corbett and his dog Pickles, who found it in a parcel abandoned under a hedge in suburban London. Brazil's third tournament victory, in 1970, entitled them to keep the trophy. In 1983, however, the trophy was stolen. It has never been recovered. Rumours suggest that it was melted down by the thieves.

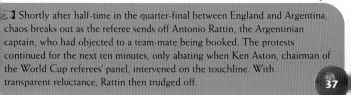

Shortly after half-time in the quarter-final between England and Argentina, chaos breaks out as the referee sends off Antonio Rattin, the Argentinian captain, who had objected to a team-mate being booked. The protests continued for the next ten minutes, only abating when Ken Aston, chairman of the World Cup referees' panel, intervened on the touchline. With transparent reluctance, Rattin then trudged off.

## Quarter-finals

England 1 Argentina 0
Portugal 5 North Korea 3

West Germany 4 Uruguay 0
Soviet Union 2 Hungary 1

## Semi-finals

West Germany 2 Soviet Union 1

England 2 Portugal 1

## Third place

Portugal 2 Soviet Union 1

## Final

England 4 West Germany 2 after extra time

### orld Cup facts

**Most red cards in a single World Cup finals match**
3   Hungary v Brazil, 1954
3   South Africa v Denmark, 1998

### orld Cup facts

**Most victories in the final by a team**
5   Brazil

### orld Cup facts

**Most goals in one tournament**
13 Just Fontaine (France), 1958

### orld Cup facts

**Most matches won in World Cup tournaments**
64 Brazil

The exhausted England centre-half Jack Charlton slumps to the ground at the end of extra time during England's climactic 4–2 victory over West Germany. Tall and rugged, he had risen to prominence under the ruthless club management of Don Revie, who guided unfashionable Leeds United to the upper reaches of English football. Charlton provided a no-nonsense contrast to his brother Bobby and to his defensive partner, Bobby Moore, arguably two of the greatest players ever to wear an England shirt.

**Most appearances in semi-final/last four**
11 Germany/West Germany

**Most matches lost in finals tournaments**
22 Mexico

**First World Cup to feature British teams**
1950. Partly due to a reluctance to play
countries with which they had recently
been at war, the British football
associations had withdrawn from FIFA in
1920.

**Number of times a non-European nation
has won a World Cup staged in Europe**
1 Brazil, 1958 in Sweden

**Number of times a European nation has won a
World Cup staged outside Europe**
0

For the 1974 World Cup finals
Argentina called up a player with
English ancestry—the
wonderfully named Carlos
Babington, who had nearly
signed for Stoke City. Such was
his delight at being called up,
Babington slept in his Argentina
shirt on the eve of his stupendous
debut against Italy in the first
round of the tournament.

**Fewest matches played in finals**
1 Dutch East Indies/Indonesia

England goalkeeper Gordon Banks (left) and defender Ray Wilson (right)
walk round the pitch after their World Cup final victory. Recognised as the
greatest goalkeeper of his generation, Banks went on to play in the 1970
tournament. His career as a top-class player was, however, brought to a
premature end when he lost an eye in a car crash.

# 1970 *Mexico*

## Group 1

| | | | | | | | |
|---|---|---|---|---|---|---|---|
| Mexico 0 Soviet Union 0 | | | | Belgium 3 El Salvador 0 | | | |
| Soviet Union 4 Belgium 1 | | | | Mexico 4 El Salvador 0 | | | |
| Soviet Union 2 El Salvador 0 | | | | Mexico 1 Belgium 0 | | | |

| | P | W | D | L | F | A | Pts |
|---|---|---|---|---|---|---|---|
| Soviet Union | 3 | 2 | 1 | 0 | 6 | 1 | 5 |
| Mexico | 3 | 2 | 1 | 0 | 5 | 0 | 5 |
| Belgium | 3 | 1 | 0 | 2 | 4 | 5 | 2 |
| El Salvador | 3 | 0 | 0 | 3 | 0 | 9 | 0 |

## Group 2

| | | | | | | | |
|---|---|---|---|---|---|---|---|
| Uruguay 2 Israel 0 | | | | Italy 1 Sweden 0 | | | |
| Uruguay 0 Italy 0 | | | | Sweden 1 Israel 1 | | | |
| Sweden 1 Uruguay 0 | | | | Italy 0 Israel 0 | | | |

| | P | W | D | L | F | A | Pts |
|---|---|---|---|---|---|---|---|
| Italy | 3 | 1 | 2 | 0 | 1 | 0 | 4 |
| Uruguay | 3 | 1 | 1 | 1 | 2 | 1 | 3 |
| Sweden | 3 | 1 | 1 | 1 | 2 | 2 | 3 |
| Israel | 3 | 0 | 2 | 1 | 1 | 3 | 2 |

## strange but true

A bottle of Mexican beer made a key contribution to England's quarter-final defeat by West Germany in the 1970 World Cup finals. Soon after drinking the beer, Gordon Banks—at that time the world's finest goalkeeper—was taken ill. His place went to the Chelsea goalkeeper, Peter 'The Cat' Bonetti, whose mistakes transformed the match.

During Brazil's 4–1 opening-round win over Czechoslovakia, the Czech goalkeeper, Ivo Viktor, shepherds the ball past the post after an audacious long-range chip by Pelé. It was a moment that encapsulated the visionary brilliance of the South American maestro, for whom the 1970 World Cup finals offered a memorable swansong.

## Group 3

England 1 Romania 0
Romania 2 Czechoslovakia 1
Brazil 3 Romania 2

Brazil 4 Czechoslovakia 1
Brazil 1 England 0
England 1 Czechoslovakia 0

|  | P | W | D | L | F | A | Pts |
|---|---|---|---|---|---|---|---|
| Brazil | 3 | 3 | 0 | 0 | 8 | 3 | 6 |
| England | 3 | 2 | 0 | 1 | 2 | 1 | 4 |
| Romania | 3 | 1 | 0 | 2 | 4 | 5 | 2 |
| Czechoslovakia | 3 | 0 | 0 | 3 | 2 | 7 | 0 |

## Group 4

Peru 3 Bulgaria 2
Peru 3 Morocco 0
West Germany 3 Peru 1

West Germany 2 Morocco 1
West Germany 5 Bulgaria 2
Morocco 1 Bulgaria 1

|  | P | W | D | L | F | A | Pts |
|---|---|---|---|---|---|---|---|
| West Germany | 3 | 3 | 0 | 0 | 10 | 4 | 6 |
| Peru | 3 | 2 | 0 | 1 | 7 | 5 | 4 |
| Bulgaria | 3 | 0 | 1 | 2 | 5 | 9 | 1 |
| Morocco | 3 | 0 | 1 | 2 | 2 | 6 | 1 |

## trange but true

The build-up to England's unsuccessful 1970 World Cup defence was marred by the arrest of Bobby Moore on a fabricated charge of stealing a bracelet. His arrest had occurred while the team was acclimatising to high-altitude conditions in Columbia. After British diplomats put pressure on the Columbian government, Moore was bailed to travel to Mexico for the World Cup finals. The criminal charge was later dropped.

England captain Bobby Moore (left) backtracks before skilfully dispossessing the Brazilian forward Jairzinho in the penalty area. Replays of Moore's tackle are frequently used to demonstrate the art of defending. But Moore's heroics couldn't prevent England from suffering a 1–0 defeat in this opening-round meeting between the World Cup holders and the previous holders. Played in searing heat, the match was notable for an exceptional save pulled off by England goalkeeper Gordon Banks. As the crowd rose to acclaim a goal, headed downwards in textbook style by Pelé, Banks dived, stretched out a hand and flipped the ball over the bar.

45

West Germany 3 England 2 after extra time | Brazil 4 Peru 2
Italy 4 Mexico 1 | Uruguay 1 Soviet Union 0 after extra time

**Semi-finals**

Italy 4 West Germany 3 after extra time | Brazil 3 Uruguay 1

**Third place**

West Germany 1 Uruguay 0

**Final**

Brazil 4 Italy 1

## strange but true

The qualifying competition for the 1970 World Cup was widely blamed for the outbreak of the so-called 'Soccer War' between El Salvador and Honduras. In June 1969 the two countries, already involved in a series of bitter political disputes, faced each other in the semi-final, played on a home and away basis. During the inconclusive second leg, held in El Salvador, Honduran fans were pelted with stones and water-bombs. The following day paramilitary groups in Honduras took revenge by evicting Salvadoran peasants from the land they'd farmed for decades. Just over two weeks after El Salvador had won the resulting play-off, sensibly staged in neutral Mexico, the Salvadoran army invaded Honduras. Though the war lasted only four days, it resulted in 1200 deaths. Most of the victims were civilians.

## orld Cup facts

**First substitute to appear in the finals** Anatoli Pusatch for the Soviet Union v Mexico, 1970. Substitutes were first introduced during that tournament.

◻ Despite his second-half goal, the midfielder Teófilo Cubillas couldn't save the gifted Peru side from a 4–2 quarter-final defeat by Brazil. Endowed with pace and superb technique, Cubillas scored ten goals in the 1970 and 1978 World Cup finals. As well as once being named 'South American Footballer of the Year', he was among the stars named in 1994 by Pelé as the '125 Greatest Living Footballers'.

47

Having beaten El Salvador in the semi-finals of
the qualifying competition for the 1970 World
Cup, El Salvador played Haiti for the right to
appear in the main part of the tournament.
Continuing their good form, the El Salvadoran
team registered a 2–1 win in the first leg. Now
they needed only a draw to qualify for the finals.
In the build-up to the game, the Haitians hired a
witchdoctor, who sprinkled a special powder on
the pitch and chanted a spell. The ensuing
Haitian victory meant that a play-off fixture had
to be arranged between the two teams. This took
place in Kingston, Jamaica. Shortly after El
Salvador scored the winning goal in extra time,
their Argentine coach, Gregorio Bundio,
celebrated by punching the witchdoctor.

As part of their training regime, the brilliant Hungarian team
which competed in the 1954 World Cup finals was encouraged
to practice not only athletics but also mountaineering.

**Most meetings between two teams**
7   Brazil v Sweden (1938, 1950, 1958, 1978, 1990 and twice in 1994)

◄ Roberto Boninsegna celebrates his equaliser for Italy in the final against
Brazil. Fielding what's widely regarded as the greatest international line-up, the
Brazilians went on to win 4–1. While the Italians pursued cautious, often
ineffective tactics, Brazil played sinuous, inventive football, orchestrated by
Gerson, Carlos Alberto, Rivelino, Jairzinho and Pelé, playing in his second
World Cup final. Soon afterwards he announced his retirement from
international football.

# 1974 *West Germany*

## Group 1

West Germany 1 Chile 0
West Germany 3 Australia 0
East Germany 1 West Germany 0

Australia 0 East Germany 2
Chile 1 East Germany 1
Chile 0 Australia 0

|  | P | W | D | L | F | A | Pts |
|---|---|---|---|---|---|---|---|
| East Germany | 3 | 2 | 1 | 0 | 4 | 1 | 5 |
| West Germany | 3 | 2 | 0 | 1 | 4 | 1 | 4 |
| Chile | 3 | 0 | 2 | 1 | 1 | 2 | 2 |
| Australia | 3 | 0 | 1 | 2 | 0 | 5 | 1 |

## Group 2

Brazil 0 Yugoslavia 0
Brazil 0 Scotland 0
Scotland 1 Yugoslavia 1

Scotland 2 Zaire 0
Yugoslavia 9 Zaire 0
Brazil 3 Zaire 0

|  | P | W | D | L | F | A | Pts |
|---|---|---|---|---|---|---|---|
| Yugoslavia | 3 | 1 | 2 | 0 | 10 | 1 | 4 |
| Brazil | 3 | 1 | 2 | 0 | 3 | 0 | 4 |
| Scotland | 3 | 1 | 2 | 0 | 3 | 1 | 4 |
| Zaire | 3 | 0 | 0 | 3 | 0 | 14 | 0 |

## World Cup facts

**The shortest World Cup finals career**
2 mins   Khemais Labidi (Tunisia), v Mexico, 1978
2 mins   Marcelo Trobbiani (Argentina), v West Germany, 1986

The rugged Manchester United centre-back Jim Holton during a brief lull in the opening stages of Scotland's anti-climactic opening-round game against outsiders Zaire. Scotland, fielding an experienced team that included Billy Bremner and Joe Jordan, struggled to a 2–0 win. 'Let's face it, we underestimated them,' Holton admitted. 'For the first fifteen minutes I wondered what the hell was going on, where the devil had this lot come from, playing stuff like that.' Even though Scotland remained unbeaten throughout the opening group stage, they failed to qualify for the next stage of the tournament.

## Group 3

| Holland 2 Uruguay 0 | Sweden 0 Bulgaria 0 |
| Holland 0 Sweden 0 | Bulgaria 1 Uruguay 1 |
| Holland 4 Bulgaria 1 | Sweden 3 Uruguay 0 |

|          | P | W | D | L | F | A | Pts |
|----------|---|---|---|---|---|---|-----|
| Holland  | 3 | 2 | 1 | 0 | 6 | 1 | 5   |
| Sweden   | 3 | 1 | 2 | 0 | 3 | 0 | 4   |
| Bulgaria | 3 | 0 | 2 | 1 | 2 | 5 | 2   |
| Uruguay  | 3 | 0 | 1 | 2 | 1 | 6 | 1   |

## Group 4

| Italy 3 Haiti 1 | Poland 3 Argentina 2 |
| Italy 1 Argentina 1 | Poland 7 Haiti 0 |
| Argentina 4 Haiti 1 | Poland 2 Italy 1 |

|           | P | W | D | L | F  | A  | Pts |
|-----------|---|---|---|---|----|----|-----|
| Poland    | 3 | 3 | 0 | 0 | 12 | 3  | 6   |
| Argentina | 3 | 1 | 1 | 1 | 7  | 5  | 3   |
| Italy     | 3 | 1 | 1 | 1 | 5  | 4  | 3   |
| Haiti     | 3 | 0 | 0 | 3 | 2  | 14 | 0   |

### orld Cup facts

**Most goals scored by a team in a World Cup finals match**
10 Hungary, v El Salvador, 1982 (El Salvador scored 1 in reply)

### orld Cup facts

**Men who won the World Cup as coaches and players**
Mário Zagallo (Brazil) won in 1958 and 1962 as a player, in 1970 as coach
Franz Beckenbauer (West Germany) won in 1974 as a player, in 1990 as coach

West German manager Helmut Schön watches his side's second game in the opening round of the tournament. Fresh from a lacklustre performance against Australia, the West Germans played Communist East Germany for the first time, political tensions reflected in the level of security at the match. Armed police kept watch over the crowd and helicopters circled the ground. The day's most shocking event turned out to be the result, a goal from Jurgen Sparwasser eight minutes from full-time securing an East German victory. Schön found himself the target of abuse, yet defeat ensured that his side avoided the powerful Dutch team in the next round. By then, the West German manager had incorporated Rainer Bonhof, Borussia Mönchengladbach's attacking midfielder, into the team which would eventually confound its critics by winning the competition.

| | | | | | | |
|---|---|---|---|---|---|---|
| Brazil 1 East Germany 0 | | | | Holland 4 Argentina 0 | | |
| Holland 2 East Germany 0 | | | | Brazil 2 Argentina 1 | | |
| Holland 2 Brazil 0 | | | | Argentina 1 East Germany 1 | | |

| | P | W | D | L | F | A | Pts |
|---|---|---|---|---|---|---|---|
| Holland | 3 | 3 | 0 | 0 | 8 | 0 | 6 |
| Brazil | 3 | 2 | 0 | 1 | 3 | 3 | 4 |
| East Germany | 3 | 0 | 1 | 2 | 1 | 4 | 1 |
| Argentina | 3 | 0 | 1 | 2 | 2 | 7 | 1 |

| | | | | | | |
|---|---|---|---|---|---|---|
| Poland 1 Sweden 0 | | | | Poland 2 Yugoslavia 1 | | |
| West Germany 2 Yugoslavia 0 | | | | West Germany 4 Sweden 2 | | |
| Sweden 2 Yugoslavia 1 | | | | West Germany 1 Poland 0 | | |

| | P | W | D | L | F | A | Pts |
|---|---|---|---|---|---|---|---|
| West Germany | 3 | 3 | 0 | 0 | 7 | 2 | 6 |
| Poland | 3 | 2 | 0 | 1 | 3 | 2 | 4 |
| Sweden | 3 | 1 | 0 | 2 | 4 | 6 | 2 |
| Yugoslavia | 3 | 0 | 0 | 3 | 2 | 6 | 0 |

Poland 1 Brazil 0

West Germany 2 Holland 1

### World Cup facts

**The only man to coach five different countries in successive finals**
Bora Milutinovic (Mexico 1986, Costa Rica 1990, USA 1994, Nigeria 1998 and China 2002). He took every team apart from China through to the second phase of the competition.

◀ Following his virtuoso display in the 0–0 opening-round draw against Sweden, Holland's Johan Cruyff is waylaid by a press photographer. This result highlighted the absence of a world-class striker to convert the opportunities created by Cruyff and his team-mates whose free-flowing style came to be known as 'total football'. Based on the premise that every outfield player should be capable of swapping positions with every other outfield player within the team, it had been pioneered by the European Cup holders, Ajax. Not since the 1970 Brazilians had there been such a beguiling demonstration of what Pelé called 'the beautiful game'.

**Only years in which the World Cup finals haven't been played**
1942 and 1946

**Most appearances in a World Cup final**
7  Brazil
7  West Germany/Germany

Near the end of the match between France and Kuwait during the 1982 finals, someone on the terraces blew a whistle. Assuming that the referee had blown for a foul, the Kuwaiti defence stopped playing. When the French player Alain Giresse scored, the referee awarded a goal, triggering a vehement protest by the Kuwaiti team. Their president, who was watching from the stands, appeared to beckon them off the field. As they were poised to troop off in disgust, he changed his mind and persuaded them to continue the game. Suddenly the referee decided to disallow the goal.

Argentina's Claudio Caniggia achieved a World Cup first in his country's match against Sweden in the 2002 finals when he was shown a red card while on the bench.

**The oldest starting line-up**
Average age of 31 years, 345 days, Germany v Iran, 1998

Alex Villaplane, captain of the French team during the 1930 World Cup finals, later collaborated with the Nazis, for which he was executed by the French Resistance.

The diminutive 32-year-old Scotland captain Billy Bremner, whose temperament was as fiery as his hair, lines up alongside centre-forward Joe Jordan before kick-off in the match against Brazil. Bremner, who helped his team-mates restrict the World Cup holders to a 0–0 draw, emerged as one of the stars of the tournament, winning the praise of Pelé and others.

# 1978 *Argentina*

## Group 1

Argentina 2 Hungary 1
Argentina 2 France 1
Argentina 0 Italy 1

France 1 Italy 2
Italy 3 Hungary 1
France 3 Hungary 1

| | P | W | D | L | F | A | Pts |
|---|---|---|---|---|---|---|---|
| Italy | 3 | 3 | 0 | 0 | 6 | 2 | 6 |
| Argentina | 3 | 2 | 0 | 1 | 4 | 3 | 4 |
| France | 3 | 1 | 0 | 2 | 5 | 5 | 2 |
| Hungary | 3 | 0 | 0 | 3 | 3 | 8 | 0 |

## Group 2

West Germany 0 Poland 0
Poland 3 Mexico 1
West Germany 0 Tunisia 0

Tunisia 3 Mexico 1
West Germany 6 Mexico 0
Poland 1 Tunisia 0

| | P | W | D | L | F | A | Pts |
|---|---|---|---|---|---|---|---|
| Poland | 3 | 2 | 1 | 0 | 4 | 1 | 5 |
| West Germany | 3 | 1 | 2 | 0 | 6 | 0 | 4 |
| Tunisia | 3 | 1 | 1 | 1 | 3 | 2 | 3 |
| Mexico | 3 | 0 | 0 | 3 | 2 | 12 | 0 |

## range but true

Henri Michel, the Frenchman who managed Cameroon's 1994 World Cup finals squad, experienced one of the most painful pre-tournament send-offs. When he arrived at Orly Airport in Paris, where he was due to board a plane to America, he was met by Jean-Claude Pagal, a member of the Cameroon squad that had been so successful in 1990. Angered at being left out of the 1994 line-up, he assaulted his former manager.

Fans in the River Plate Stadium, Buenos Aires were treated by the highly rated West German and Polish teams to one of the dullest opening matches in World Cup history. This unpromising start heralded a tournament scarred by refereeing controversies, by the triumphalism of the ruling Argentine military junta, and by the failure of the football to live up to the standard set by the 1974 finals.

## Group 3

Austria 2 Spain 1
Austria 1 Sweden 0
Spain 1 Sweden 0

Sweden 1 Brazil 1
Spain 0 Brazil 0
Brazil 1 Austria 0

|         | P | W | D | L | F | A | Pts |
|---------|---|---|---|---|---|---|-----|
| Austria | 3 | 2 | 0 | 1 | 3 | 2 | 4   |
| Brazil  | 3 | 1 | 2 | 0 | 2 | 1 | 4   |
| Spain   | 3 | 1 | 1 | 1 | 2 | 2 | 3   |
| Sweden  | 3 | 0 | 1 | 2 | 3 | 3 | 1   |

## Group 4

Scotland 1 Peru 3
Scotland 1 Iran 1
Peru 4 Iran 1

Holland 3 Iran 0
Holland 0 Peru 0
Scotland 3 Holland 2

|          | P | W | D | L | F | A | Pts |
|----------|---|---|---|---|---|---|-----|
| Peru     | 3 | 2 | 1 | 0 | 7 | 2 | 5   |
| Holland  | 3 | 1 | 1 | 1 | 5 | 3 | 3   |
| Scotland | 3 | 1 | 1 | 1 | 5 | 6 | 3   |
| Iran     | 3 | 0 | 1 | 2 | 2 | 8 | 1   |

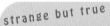

### strange but true

Just over a year before the 1978 World Cup finals, West Germany's captain and star player Franz Beckenbaur opted out of the tournament by accepting a $2.5 million offer to play for the New York Cosmos.

### World Cup facts

**Most meetings between two teams in the final**
2  Brazil v Italy (1970 and 1994)
2  Argentina v West Germany (1986 and 1990)

Two indignant Brazilian players confront Welsh referee Clive Thomas, who has just disallowed a goal during the final seconds of the opening-round draw with Sweden. Thomas had blown the full-time whistle moments before Zico, rising to meet a corner, had headed the ball into the net. So controversial was the decision that Thomas would never be allowed to referee another World Cup game. Zico and his team, among them the overweight Rivelino, meanwhile staggered through to the competition's knockout stages where they displayed some of the anticipated flair.

## Group A

| | | | | | | | |
|---|---|---|---|---|---|---|---|
Italy 0 West Germany 0 | | | | Holland 5 Austria 1 | | | |
Italy 1 Austria 0 | | | | Austria 3 West Germany 2 | | | |
Holland 2 Italy 1 | | | | West Germany 2 Holland 2 | | | |

| | P | W | D | L | F | A | Pts |
|---|---|---|---|---|---|---|---|
| Holland | 3 | 2 | 1 | 0 | 9 | 4 | 5 |
| Italy | 3 | 1 | 1 | 1 | 2 | 2 | 3 |
| West Germany | 3 | 0 | 2 | 1 | 4 | 5 | 2 |
| Austria | 3 | 1 | 0 | 2 | 4 | 8 | 2 |

## Group B

| | | | | | | | |
|---|---|---|---|---|---|---|---|
Poland 0 Argentina 2 | | | | Brazil 3 Peru 0 | | | |
Brazil 0 Argentina 0 | | | | Poland 1 Peru 0 | | | |
Brazil 3 Poland 1 | | | | Argentina 6 Peru 0 | | | |

| | P | W | D | L | F | A | Pts |
|---|---|---|---|---|---|---|---|
| Argentina | 3 | 2 | 1 | 0 | 8 | 0 | 5 |
| Brazil | 3 | 2 | 1 | 0 | 6 | 1 | 5 |
| Poland | 3 | 1 | 0 | 2 | 2 | 5 | 2 |
| Peru | 3 | 0 | 0 | 3 | 0 | 10 | 0 |

## Third place

Brazil 2 Italy 1

## Final

Argentina 3 Holland 1 after extra time

### World Cup facts

**Players most frequently sent off**
2 Rigobert Song (Cameroon), v
  Brazil (1994), v Chile (1998)
2 Zinedine Zidane (France), v Saudi
  Arabia (1998), v Italy (2006)

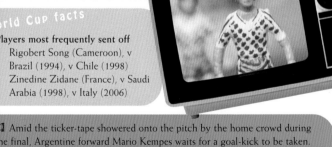

Amid the ticker-tape showered onto the pitch by the home crowd during the final, Argentine forward Mario Kempes waits for a goal-kick to be taken. The pacey and energetic Kempes, who had established himself as the leading striker in La Liga, was one of a group of top Argentine players who had signed for European clubs, in his case Valencia. But their country's chain-smoking new manager, César Luis Menotti, insisted on picking only three of them—a trio that included Kempes. Even though the Dutch decided to man-mark him, he scored twice, earning himself national-hero status.

# 1982 *Spain*

| | | | | | | | |
|---|---|---|---|---|---|---|---|
| Italy 0 Poland 0 | | | | Cameroon 0 Peru 0 | | | |
| Italy 1 Peru 1 | | | | Poland 0 Cameroon 0 | | | |
| Poland 5 Peru 1 | | | | Italy 1 Cameroon 1 | | | |

| | P | W | D | L | F | A | Pts |
|---|---|---|---|---|---|---|---|
| Poland | 3 | 1 | 2 | 0 | 5 | 1 | 4 |
| Italy | 3 | 0 | 3 | 0 | 2 | 2 | 3 |
| Cameroon | 3 | 0 | 3 | 0 | 1 | 1 | 3 |
| Peru | 3 | 0 | 2 | 1 | 2 | 6 | 2 |

| | | | | | | | |
|---|---|---|---|---|---|---|---|
| West Germany 1 Algeria 2 | | | | Austria 1 Chile 0 | | | |
| West Germany 4 Chile 1 | | | | Austria 2 Algeria 0 | | | |
| Algeria 3 Chile 2 | | | | West Germany 1 Austria 0 | | | |

| | P | W | D | L | F | A | Pts |
|---|---|---|---|---|---|---|---|
| West Germany | 3 | 2 | 0 | 1 | 6 | 3 | 4 |
| Austria | 3 | 2 | 0 | 1 | 3 | 1 | 4 |
| Algeria | 3 | 2 | 0 | 1 | 5 | 5 | 4 |
| Chile | 3 | 0 | 0 | 3 | 3 | 8 | 0 |

◀ Pat Jennings (left), the Northern Ireland goalkeeper, in his team's surprise 1–0 opening-round win over Spain. It was a victory achieved against an apparently far superior Spanish side. Nowhere was the gap in class more evident than in the presence of goalscorer Gerry Armstrong, who had struggled to break into the team at Second Division Watford. The chances of a Northern Irish victory were further diminished by the conditions in which the fixture was played. Not only did the Spanish have the advantage of a hostile home crowd, they were also more accustomed to the prevailing heat, so severe that it left at least one Irish player severely dehydrated. On top of all that, the Paraguayan referee—who had previously ignored numerous heavy tackles—sent off the Irish defender Willie Donaghy. The victory earned a place in the next round.

## Group 3

Argentina 0 Belgium 1
Argentina 4 Hungary 1
Belgium 1 Hungary 1

El Salvador 1 Hungary 10
El Salvador 0 Belgium 1
Argentina 2 El Salvador 0

|  | P | W | D | L | F | A | Pts |
|---|---|---|---|---|---|---|---|
| Belgium | 3 | 2 | 1 | 0 | 3 | 1 | 5 |
| Argentina | 3 | 2 | 0 | 1 | 6 | 2 | 4 |
| Hungary | 3 | 1 | 1 | 1 | 12 | 6 | 3 |
| El Salvador | 3 | 0 | 0 | 3 | 1 | 13 | 0 |

## Group 4

England 3 France 1
England 2 Czechoslovakia 0
France 1 Czechoslovakia 1

Czechoslovakia 1 Kuwait 1
France 4 Kuwait 1
England 1 Kuwait 0

|  | P | W | D | L | F | A | Pts |
|---|---|---|---|---|---|---|---|
| England | 3 | 3 | 0 | 0 | 6 | 1 | 6 |
| France | 3 | 1 | 1 | 1 | 6 | 5 | 3 |
| Czechoslovakia | 3 | 0 | 2 | 1 | 2 | 4 | 2 |
| Kuwait | 3 | 0 | 1 | 2 | 2 | 6 | 1 |

## Group 5

Honduras 1 Spain 1
Spain 2 Yugoslavia 1
Honduras 0 Yugoslavia 1

Yugoslavia 0 Northern Ireland 0
Honduras 1 Northern Ireland 1
Spain 0 Northern Ireland 1

|  | P | W | D | L | F | A | Pts |
|---|---|---|---|---|---|---|---|
| Northern Ireland | 3 | 1 | 2 | 0 | 2 | 1 | 4 |
| Spain | 3 | 1 | 1 | 1 | 3 | 3 | 3 |
| Yugoslavia | 3 | 1 | 1 | 1 | 2 | 2 | 3 |
| Honduras | 3 | 0 | 2 | 1 | 2 | 3 | 2 |

## Group 6

Brazil 2 Soviet Union 1
Brazil 4 Scotland 1
Scotland 2 Soviet Union 2

New Zealand 2 Scotland 5
Soviet Union 3 New Zealand 0
Brazil 4 New Zealand 0

|  | P | W | D | L | F | A | Pts |
|---|---|---|---|---|---|---|---|
| Brazil | 3 | 3 | 0 | 0 | 10 | 2 | 6 |
| Soviet Union | 3 | 1 | 1 | 1 | 6 | 4 | 3 |
| Scotland | 3 | 1 | 1 | 1 | 8 | 8 | 3 |
| New Zealand | 3 | 0 | 0 | 3 | 2 | 12 | 0 |

Grim-faced New Zealand substitutes watch their team's 5–2 drubbing by Scotland. It was the first of three heavy defeats that saw the team, which had never previously qualified for the World Cup finals, concede a dozen goals. The Kiwis' predictably poor performance did little to help football challenge the dominance of rugby union and cricket in New Zealand.

Poland 3 Belgium 0                  Belgium 0 Soviet Union 1
Soviet Union 0 Poland 0

|  | P | W | D | L | F | A | Pts |
|---|---|---|---|---|---|---|---|
| Poland | 2 | 1 | 1 | 0 | 3 | 0 | 3 |
| Soviet Union | 2 | 1 | 1 | 0 | 1 | 0 | 3 |
| Belgium | 2 | 0 | 0 | 2 | 0 | 4 | 0 |

### Group B

West Germany 0 England 0             Spain 1 West Germany 2
Spain 0 England 0

|  | P | W | D | L | F | A | Pts |
|---|---|---|---|---|---|---|---|
| West Germany | 2 | 1 | 1 | 0 | 2 | 1 | 3 |
| England | 2 | 0 | 2 | 0 | 0 | 0 | 2 |
| Spain | 2 | 0 | 1 | 1 | 1 | 2 | 1 |

## World Cup facts

**Youngest player in the finals**
17 years, 41 days Norman Whiteside (Northern Ireland) v Yugoslavia, 1982

## World Cup facts

**Most appearances by a team without advancing beyond the first round**
8 Scotland

Brazilian captain and midfielder Sócrates Brasileiro Sampaio de Souza Vieira de Oliveira, usually known as Sócrates, enjoys a cigarette during a training session, watched by thousands of admiring fans. Despite being a heavy smoker, he was one of his country's greatest midfielders, playing with a distinctively languid, loping style. The 1982 Brazilian World Cup squad is often cited as one of the most talented group of players not to have won the competition. Most of Sócrates's club football was played for the São Paulo-based club Corinthians, where he co-founded the Corinthians' Democracy Movement, which protested against the ruling Brazilian military dictatorship. As well as enjoying a distinguished sporting career, he also qualified as a doctor of medicine.

## Group C

Italy 2 Argentina 1
Brazil 2 Italy 3

Argentina 1 Brazil 3

|  | P | W | D | L | F | A | Pts |
|---|---|---|---|---|---|---|---|
| Italy | 2 | 2 | 0 | 0 | 5 | 3 | 4 |
| Brazil | 2 | 1 | 0 | 1 | 5 | 4 | 2 |
| Argentina | 2 | 0 | 0 | 2 | 2 | 5 | 0 |

## Group D

France 1 Austria 0
France 4 Northern Ireland 1

Northern Ireland 2 Austria 2

|  | P | W | D | L | F | A | Pts |
|---|---|---|---|---|---|---|---|
| France | 2 | 2 | 0 | 0 | 5 | 1 | 4 |
| Austria | 2 | 0 | 1 | 1 | 2 | 3 | 1 |
| Northern Ireland | 2 | 0 | 1 | 1 | 3 | 6 | 1 |

## Semi-finals

Italy 2 Poland 0

France 3 West Germany 3 after extra time (West Germany won on penalties)

## Third place

Poland 3 France 2

## Final

Italy 3 West Germany 1

## trange but true

In the first round of the 1982 World Cup finals, West Germany and Austria played what was widely regarded as a rigged game. The Germans won 1–0, ensuring that Austria qualified for the next phase in place of Algeria.

▶ In what would be the turning-point of one of the World Cup's most exciting semi-finals, French substitute Patrick Battiston (left) races towards the West German goalkeeper Harald Schumacher (right). Unleashed by a perfectly judged through-ball, Battiston had the chance to net the winning goal, but Schumacher ignored the ball and instead concentrated on flattening the French player with a forearm smash. The force of the blow knocked out two of Battiston's teeth and left him unconscious on the pitch, so seriously injured that he could have died. The referee, who claimed not to have seen the incident, failed to send off Schumacher or to award a penalty. France went on to lose the game.

One of the least eventful matches in World Cup history took place in October 1996 when Scotland was due to play Estonia in Tallinn. In the days leading up to the fixture, Scottish officials complained about the temporary floodlighting provided for the match. Siding with Scotland, FIFA insisted that the kick-off time should be changed from the evening to the afternoon, avoiding the need to use floodlights. As a protest, the Estonian team failed to turn up for the match, prompting the Scottish fans to chant, 'There's only one team in Tallinn…' No sooner had the Scottish midfielder John Collins kicked off than the referee blew the full-time whistle. In line with the FIFA ruling on teams that failed to turn up for matches, a 3–0 victory was awarded to Scotland. Under pressure from the Estonians, however, FIFA eventually modified their rules and made the two teams play the game on a neutral ground. Despite emerging from the match with only a 0–0 draw, Scotland still succeeded in qualifying for the 1998 World Cup finals.

## orld Cup facts

**Only time an unbeaten team has failed to reach the second round**
Scotland, 1974

◄ Marco Tardelli runs across the pitch at the Bernabéu in the ecstatic aftermath of scoring the second goal in Italy's 3–1 win over West Germany in the final. At the start of the tournament few people had anticipated an Italian win. After three disjointed performances in the opening round, the team remained unfancied. Just as West Germany had done on so many previous occasions, the 'azzuri' became much more formidable with each subsequent game. The catalyst for this surprising transformation was the boyish-looking striker Paolo Rossi, whose involvement in a betting scandal had led to him receiving a three-year suspension. That had been controversially reduced, enabling him to play in the tournament. At first he appeared understandably rusty, but by the final he had recaptured the form that had earned him a reputation as one of Europe's sharpest goal-poachers.

# 1986 *Mexico*

## Group A

Italy 1 Bulgaria 1
Argentina 1 Italy 1
South Korea 2 Italy 3

South Korea 1 Argentina 3
Bulgaria 1 South Korea 1
Bulgaria 0 Argentina 2

|             | P | W | D | L | F | A | Pts |
|-------------|---|---|---|---|---|---|-----|
| Argentina   | 3 | 2 | 1 | 0 | 6 | 2 | 5   |
| Italy       | 3 | 1 | 2 | 0 | 5 | 4 | 4   |
| Bulgaria    | 3 | 0 | 2 | 1 | 2 | 4 | 2   |
| South Korea | 3 | 0 | 1 | 2 | 4 | 7 | 1   |

## Group B

Mexico 2 Belgium 1
Mexico 1 Paraguay 1
Mexico 1 Iraq 0

Paraguay 1 Iraq 0
Iraq 1 Belgium 2
Belgium 2 Paraguay 2

|          | P | W | D | L | F | A | Pts |
|----------|---|---|---|---|---|---|-----|
| Mexico   | 3 | 2 | 1 | 0 | 4 | 2 | 5   |
| Paraguay | 3 | 1 | 2 | 0 | 4 | 3 | 4   |
| Belgium  | 3 | 1 | 1 | 1 | 5 | 5 | 3   |
| Iraq     | 3 | 0 | 0 | 3 | 1 | 4 | 0   |

### World Cup facts

**Player with most World Cup winners' medals**
3   Pelé (1958, 1962, 1970)

England centre-forward, Mark Hateley, pictured during his country's 3–0 defeat of Paraguay in the second round. Managed by Bobby Robson, who would later coach Barcelona and PSV Eindhoven, England had only just sneaked into the World Cup finals after a draw against Northern Ireland—a result that had edged out the Romanians. Against this background, Robson's side went into the tournament with little optimism. After an opening-round draw and a defeat, England was in danger of being knocked out of the tournament. Under pressure from his own players, Robson altered the line-up and the tactics, affecting a rapid reversal in their fortunes.

## Group C

France 1 Canada 0
Soviet Union 1 France 1
France 3 Hungary 0

Hungary 0 Soviet Union 6
Hungary 2 Canada 0
Soviet Union 2 Canada 0

| | P | W | D | L | F | A | Pts |
|---|---|---|---|---|---|---|---|
| Soviet Union | 3 | 2 | 1 | 0 | 9 | 1 | 5 |
| France | 3 | 2 | 1 | 0 | 5 | 1 | 5 |
| Hungary | 3 | 1 | 0 | 2 | 2 | 9 | 2 |
| Canada | 3 | 0 | 0 | 3 | 0 | 5 | 0 |

## Group D

Brazil 1 Spain 0
Spain 2 Northern Ireland 1
Algeria 0 Spain 3

Northern Ireland 1 Algeria 1
Brazil 1 Algeria 0
Northern Ireland 0 Brazil 3

| | P | W | D | L | F | A | Pts |
|---|---|---|---|---|---|---|---|
| Brazil | 3 | 3 | 0 | 0 | 5 | 0 | 6 |
| Spain | 3 | 2 | 0 | 1 | 5 | 2 | 4 |
| Northern Ireland | 3 | 0 | 1 | 2 | 2 | 6 | 1 |
| Algeria | 3 | 0 | 1 | 2 | 1 | 5 | 1 |

## Group E

Scotland 0 Denmark 1
Scotland 1 West Germany 2
Scotland 0 Uruguay 0

West Germany 1 Uruguay 1
Denmark 6 Uruguay 1
West Germany 0 Denmark 2

| | P | W | D | L | F | A | Pts |
|---|---|---|---|---|---|---|---|
| Denmark | 3 | 3 | 0 | 0 | 9 | 1 | 6 |
| West Germany | 3 | 1 | 1 | 1 | 3 | 4 | 3 |
| Uruguay | 3 | 0 | 2 | 1 | 2 | 7 | 2 |
| Scotland | 3 | 0 | 1 | 2 | 1 | 3 | 1 |

## orld Cup facts

**Fastest sending-off**

56 secs   Sergio Batista (Uruguay), v Scotland, 1986

◗ In the quarter-final at the Azteca Stadium, Argentina's Diego Maradona (left) punches the ball past England goalkeeper Peter Shilton. Undeterred by he vehement protests, Ali Bennaceur, the Tunisian referee, refused to disallow he goal. Not long afterwards Maradona, this time without a hint of ontroversy, scored the winning goal—a solo creation in which he slalomed ast four defenders and then the goalkeeper. In a post-match interview, Maradona cheekily referred to his hand-ball as 'the Hand of God'.

77

| | | | | | | | |
|---|---|---|---|---|---|---|---|
| Portugal 1 England 0 | | | | Morocco 0 Poland 0 | | | |
| Portugal 0 Poland 1 | | | | Morocco 0 England 0 | | | |
| Morocco 3 Portugal 1 | | | | England 3 Poland 0 | | | |

| | P | W | D | L | F | A | Pts |
|---|---|---|---|---|---|---|---|
| Morocco | 3 | 1 | 2 | 0 | 3 | 1 | 4 |
| England | 3 | 1 | 1 | 1 | 3 | 1 | 3 |
| Poland | 3 | 1 | 1 | 1 | 1 | 3 | 3 |
| Portugal | 3 | 1 | 0 | 2 | 2 | 4 | 2 |

## Second round

| | |
|---|---|
| Soviet Union 3 Belgium 4 after extra time | Mexico 2 Bulgaria 0 |
| Brazil 4 Poland 0 | Argentina 1 Uruguay 0 |
| France 2 Italy 0 | West Germany 1 Morocco 0 |
| England 3 Paraguay 0 | Denmark 1 Spain 5 |

## Quarter-finals

| | |
|---|---|
| France 1 Brazil 1 (France won on penalties) | Mexico 0 West Germany 0 (West Germany won on penalties) |
| Argentina 2 England 1 | Belgium 1 Spain 1 (Belgium won on penalties) |

## Semi-finals

| | |
|---|---|
| Belgium 0 Argentina 2 | France 0 West Germany 2 |

## Third place

Belgium 2 France 4 after extra time

## Final

Argentina 3 West Germany 2

## orld Cup facts

**World Cup winners who have successfully defended the cup**
Italy, won 1934, retained 1938
Brazil, won 1958, retained 1962

After netting Mexico's second goal in his country's 2–1 victory over Belgium, Hugo Sánchez, the Real Madrid striker, performs his customary gymnastic celebration. This goal aside, he made a negligible contribution to what turned out to be a disappointing campaign for both him and his team. Usually rated as the best-ever Mexican player, Sánchez had also failed to reproduce his prolific club form during the 1982 World Cup finals. The 1986 tournament represented his last opportunity to establish himself as a top international striker. He later had a brief, unsuccessful spell as Mexican team-manager.

During the 1994 World Cup finals, matches were played indoors for the first time, at the Pontiac Silverdome in Detroit. The grass had to be grown in California and shipped there at enormous expense.

## World Cup facts

**Most goals conceded by a team in World Cup tournaments**
112   Germany/West Germany

Peruvian Ramon Quiroga has the rare distinction for a goalkeeper of being booked in the other team's half. He regularly strayed out of his penalty-box to help Peru's defence. During their 1–0 defeat by Poland in the second round of the 1978 finals, he took this one stage further by rugby-tackling Grzegorz Lato, earning himself a yellow card.

In the 2006 World Cup finals, Oleg Blokhin, the Ukraine coach, promised that he'd waive the squad's rule on celibacy if they reached the semi-finals. 'Those who don't feel like it, I'll just drag to their wives,' he added.

So far, 20 World Cup finals matches have been decided by penalty shoot-outs. Of those, 55 per cent were won by the team taking the first penalty.

Viv Richards played in both the football and cricket World Cups. In cricket, he starred in two tournament-winning West Indies sides. In football, however, his record is less imposing. He played for Antigua in four qualifying matches for the 1974 finals. One of these was an 11–0 defeat.

Originally awarded to Colombia, the 1986 World Cup finals had been moved to Mexico when it became apparent that the crisis-ridden Colombians couldn't afford to honour their commitment. The poor quality of many of the pitches didn't stop the tournament from producing some impressive football. Just as Pelé was the dominant presence in 1970, Maradona will forever be associated with the tournament's second visit to Mexico. The 1986 finals are also inextricably associated with the so-called 'Mexican wave', seen here, though the phenomenon pre-dates 1986.

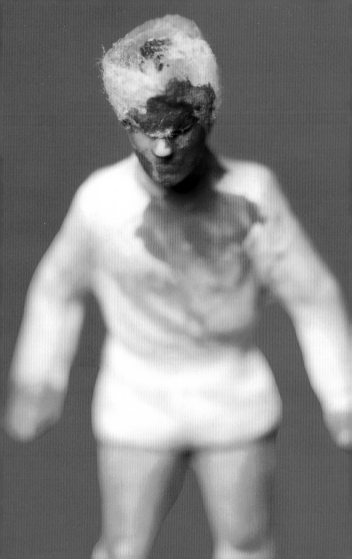

# 1990 *Italy*

## Group A

| | | | | | | | |
|---|---|---|---|---|---|---|---|
Italy 1 Austria 0 | | | | USA 1 Czechoslovakia 5 | | |
Italy 1 USA 0 | | | | Austria 0 Czechoslovakia 1 | | |
Italy 2 Czechoslovakia 0 | | | | Austria 2 USA 1 | | |

| | P | W | D | L | F | A | Pts |
|---|---|---|---|---|---|---|---|
| Italy | 3 | 3 | 0 | 0 | 4 | 0 | 6 |
| Czechoslovakia | 3 | 2 | 0 | 1 | 6 | 3 | 4 |
| Austria | 3 | 1 | 0 | 2 | 2 | 3 | 2 |
| USA | 3 | 0 | 0 | 3 | 2 | 8 | 0 |

## Group B

| | | | | | | | |
|---|---|---|---|---|---|---|---|
Cameroon 1 Argentina 0 | | | | Romania 2 Soviet Union 0 | | |
Soviet Union 0 Argentina 2 | | | | Cameroon 2 Romania 1 | | |
Argentina 1 Romania 1 | | | | Soviet Union 4 Cameroon 0 | | |

| | P | W | D | L | F | A | Pts |
|---|---|---|---|---|---|---|---|
| Cameroon | 3 | 2 | 0 | 1 | 3 | 5 | 4 |
| Romania | 3 | 1 | 1 | 1 | 4 | 3 | 3 |
| Argentina | 3 | 1 | 1 | 1 | 3 | 2 | 3 |
| Soviet Union | 3 | 1 | 0 | 2 | 4 | 4 | 2 |

## World Cup facts

Number of spectators at the worst attended World Cup qualifier
0   Costa Rica v Panama, 2006

For the 30-year-old England central defender Terry Butcher, this was the defining moment in his international career. Early in a vital World Cup qualifying game against Sweden, played during September 1989, he suffered a deep gash across his forehead. The England physiotherapist stitched the wound and bandaged it. Showing notable bravery, Butcher continued to head the ball even though the impact of each header helped to reopen the wound and dislodge the bandages. By the end of the game, his bandages had disintegrated and his England shirt was covered in his own blood. Thanks to his heroics, England obtained the required draw, enabling the team to qualify for the 1990 World Cup finals.

## Group C

| | | | | | | | |
|---|---|---|---|---|---|---|---|
| Brazil 2 Sweden 1 | | | | Scotland 0 Costa Rica 1 | | | |
| Costa Rica 0 Brazil 1 | | | | Scotland 2 Sweden 1 | | | |
| Brazil 1 Scotland 0 | | | | Costa Rica 2 Sweden 1 | | | |

| | P | W | D | L | F | A | Pts |
|---|---|---|---|---|---|---|---|
| Brazil | 3 | 3 | 0 | 0 | 4 | 1 | 6 |
| Costa Rica | 3 | 2 | 0 | 1 | 3 | 2 | 4 |
| Scotland | 3 | 1 | 0 | 2 | 2 | 3 | 2 |
| Sweden | 3 | 0 | 0 | 3 | 3 | 6 | 0 |

## Group D

| | | | | | | | |
|---|---|---|---|---|---|---|---|
| Colombia 2 United Arab Emirates 0 | | | | West Germany 4 Yugoslavia 1 | | | |
| West Germany 5 United Arab Emirates 1 | | | | Yugoslavia 1 Colombia 0 | | | |
| Yugoslavia 4 United Arab Emirates 1 | | | | Colombia 1 West Germany 1 | | | |

| | P | W | D | L | F | A | Pts |
|---|---|---|---|---|---|---|---|
| West Germany | 3 | 2 | 1 | 0 | 10 | 3 | 5 |
| Yugoslavia | 3 | 2 | 0 | 1 | 6 | 5 | 4 |
| Colombia | 3 | 1 | 1 | 1 | 3 | 2 | 3 |
| United Arab Emirates | 3 | 0 | 0 | 3 | 2 | 11 | 0 |

## Group E

| | | | | | | | |
|---|---|---|---|---|---|---|---|
| Belgium 2 South Korea 0 | | | | Spain 0 Uruguay 0 | | | |
| Spain 3 South Korea 1 | | | | Belgium 3 Uruguay 1 | | | |
| Spain 2 Belgium 1 | | | | Uruguay 1 South Korea 0 | | | |

| | P | W | D | L | F | A | Pts |
|---|---|---|---|---|---|---|---|
| Spain | 3 | 2 | 1 | 0 | 5 | 2 | 5 |
| Belgium | 3 | 2 | 0 | 1 | 6 | 3 | 4 |
| Uruguay | 3 | 1 | 1 | 1 | 2 | 3 | 3 |
| South Korea | 3 | 0 | 0 | 3 | 1 | 6 | 0 |

### World Cup facts

**Longest period a goalkeeper has remained unbeaten**

517 mins   Walter Zenga (Italy). His unbeaten run was brought to an end
when the Argentine forward Claudio Caniggia scored in the 1990
semi-final.

The notorious incident when Holland midfielder Frank Rijkaard spat at the
West German striker Rudi Völler twenty-one minutes into a bad-tempered
second-round match at the San Siro. Both players were sent off, their departure
overshadowing the brilliance of the game, which soon developed into
one of the World Cup's most thrilling encounters.

England 1 Rep. of Ireland 1
Holland 0 England 0
England 1 Egypt 0

Holland 1 Egypt 1
Egypt 0 Rep. of Ireland 0
Rep. of Ireland 1 Holland 1

| | P | W | D | L | F | A | Pts |
|---|---|---|---|---|---|---|---|
| England | 3 | 1 | 2 | 0 | 2 | 1 | 4 |
| Rep. of Ireland | 3 | 0 | 3 | 0 | 2 | 2 | 3 |
| Holland | 3 | 0 | 3 | 0 | 2 | 2 | 3 |
| Egypt | 3 | 0 | 2 | 1 | 1 | 2 | 2 |

## Second round

Cameroon 2 Colombia 1 after extra time
Argentina 1 Brazil 0
Romania 0 Rep. of Ireland 0 (Rep. of
Ireland won on penalties)
England 1 Belgium 0 after extra time

Costa Rica 1 Czechoslovakia 4
Holland 1 West Germany 2
Italy 2 Uruguay 0
Yugoslavia 2 Spain 1 after extra time

## Quarter-finals

Italy 1 Rep. of Ireland 0
England 3 Cameroon 2 after extra time

West Germany 1 Czechoslovakia 0
Argentina 0 Yugoslavia 0
(Argentina won on penalties)

## Semi-finals

Argentina 1 Italy 1 (Argentina won on penalties)
West Germany 1 England 1 (West Germany won on penalties)

## Third place

Italy 2 England 1

## Final

West Germany 1 Argentina 0

## orld Cup facts

Country with highest average of goals scored per match
2.72 Hungary

Veteran centre-half David O'Leary prepares to take the decisive penalty in the shoot-out that sent the Republic of Ireland through to the quarter-finals at the expense of Romania. An unlikely saviour, O'Leary had only been brought on in the 93rd minute. His powerful penalty sent the Irish into the quarter-finals, where their good fortune deserted them and they were beaten 1–0 by Italy.

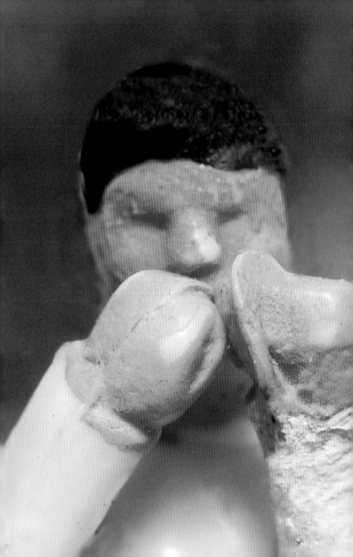

In September 1989 Brazil played Chile in a qualifying game for the 1990 World Cup. While Brazil only needed a draw, Chile had to win. With the Brazilians leading 1–0, an attempt was made by the Chileans to get the match abandoned. Just over 20 minutes of normal time remained when a green flare was thrown into the Chilean goalmouth, at which point the Chilean goalkeeper, Roberto Rojas, collapsed, clutching his face, blood apparently pouring from a wound. Instead of waiting for an official stretcher, the Chilean team carried him to the dressing-room. Claiming their lives were in danger if they continued with the game, the Chileans refused to go back onto the pitch. Though their team doctor reported that Rojas had suffered a facial wound which necessitated five stitches, photographs later revealed that the injury had been faked. FIFA suspended Rojas from international football for life. Several of the Chilean officials, including the team doctor, were also suspended. Chile was, in addition, banned from taking part in the 1994 World Cup.

## orld Cup facts

**Player who has appeared in the most finals competitions**

5   Antonio Carbajal (Mexico), 1950–66
5   Lothar Matthäus (West Germany/Germany), 1982–98

Talented England midfielder Paul 'Gazza' Gascoigne bursts into tears after being booked during England's epic semi-final against West Germany. Had his team not lost the eventual penalty shoot-out, his booking would have rendered him ineligible for the World Cup final. Only drafted into the England squad at the last minute, he nevertheless used the competition to signal his arrival as one of the world's best midfielders, blessed with an impressive first-touch and power, along with extraordinary balance and dribbling skills.

# 1994 *USA*

## Group A

| | | | | | | | |
|---|---|---|---|---|---|---|---|
USA 1 Switzerland 1 | | | | Romania 3 Colombia 1 | | | |
USA 2 Colombia 1 | | | | Switzerland 4 Romania 1 | | | |
Romania 1 USA 0 | | | | Colombia 2 Switzerland 0 | | | |

| | P | W | D | L | F | A | Pts |
|---|---|---|---|---|---|---|---|
| Romania | 3 | 2 | 0 | 1 | 5 | 5 | 6 |
| Switzerland | 3 | 1 | 1 | 1 | 5 | 4 | 4 |
| USA | 3 | 1 | 1 | 1 | 3 | 3 | 4 |
| Colombia | 3 | 1 | 0 | 2 | 4 | 5 | 3 |

## Group B

| | | | | | | | |
|---|---|---|---|---|---|---|---|
Cameroon 2 Sweden 2 | | | | Brazil 2 Russia 0 | | | |
Brazil 3 Cameroon 0 | | | | Sweden 3 Russia 1 | | | |
Brazil 1 Sweden 1 | | | | Russia 6 Cameroon 1 | | | |

| | P | W | D | L | F | A | Pts |
|---|---|---|---|---|---|---|---|
| Brazil | 3 | 2 | 1 | 0 | 6 | 1 | 7 |
| Sweden | 3 | 1 | 2 | 0 | 6 | 4 | 5 |
| Russia | 3 | 1 | 0 | 2 | 7 | 6 | 3 |
| Cameroon | 3 | 0 | 1 | 2 | 3 | 11 | 1 |

## orld Cup facts

Country that's scored most goals in finals tournaments

202  Brazil

◀ At the start of the tournament, the Colombians were being touted by Pelé among others as potential World Cup winners. The South American team certainly possessed players blessed with technical virtuosity, none more so than the flamboyant midfielder, Carlos Valderrama, seen here during his team's 3–1 opening-round defeat by Romania. But this was only the prelude to a far bigger shock. In Pasadena, the relatively unfancied US team inflicted a second consecutive defeat on the Colombians. So improbable was the result that there was considerable speculation about whether the game had been fixed. Though his team won their final opening-round match, their improved performance inspired by Valderrama, this came too late to enable them to qualify for the next stage of the tournament.

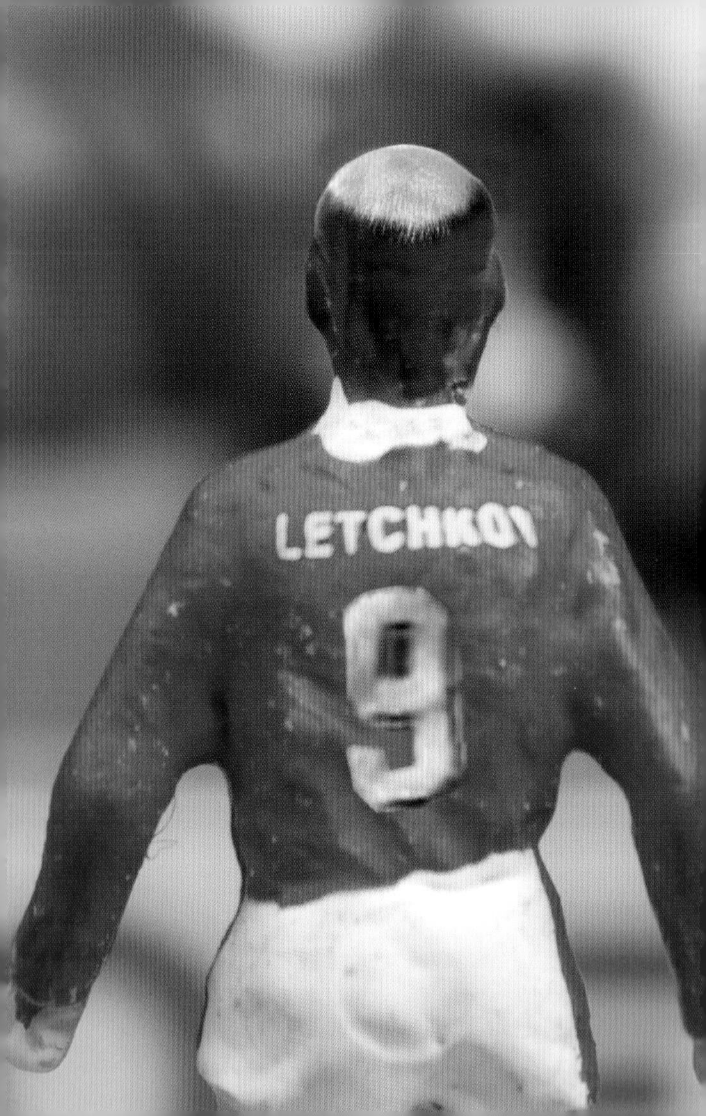
LETCHKOV
9

## Group C

| | | | | | | | |
|---|---|---|---|---|---|---|---|
Germany 1 Bolivia 0 | | | | Spain 2 South Korea 2 | | | |
Germany 1 Spain 1 | | | | Bolivia 0 South Korea 0 | | | |
Germany 3 South Korea 2 | | | | Bolivia 1 Spain 3 | | | |

| | P | W | D | L | F | A | Pts |
|---|---|---|---|---|---|---|---|
| Germany | 3 | 2 | 1 | 0 | 5 | 3 | 7 |
| Spain | 3 | 1 | 2 | 0 | 6 | 4 | 5 |
| South Korea | 3 | 0 | 2 | 1 | 4 | 5 | 2 |
| Bolivia | 3 | 0 | 1 | 2 | 1 | 4 | 1 |

## Group D

| | | | | | | | |
|---|---|---|---|---|---|---|---|
Argentina 4 Greece 0 | | | | Bulgaria 0 Nigeria 3 | | | |
Nigeria 1 Argentina 2 | | | | Bulgaria 4 Greece 0 | | | |
Argentina 0 Bulgaria 2 | | | | Greece 0 Nigeria 2 | | | |

| | P | W | D | L | F | A | Pts |
|---|---|---|---|---|---|---|---|
| Nigeria | 3 | 2 | 0 | 1 | 6 | 2 | 6 |
| Bulgaria | 3 | 2 | 0 | 1 | 6 | 3 | 6 |
| Argentina | 3 | 2 | 0 | 1 | 6 | 3 | 6 |
| Greece | 3 | 0 | 0 | 3 | 0 | 10 | 0 |

## Group E

| | | | | | | | |
|---|---|---|---|---|---|---|---|
Rep. of Ireland 1 Italy 0 | | | | Norway 1 Mexico 0 | | | |
Italy 1 Norway 0 | | | | Mexico 2 Rep. of Ireland 1 | | | |
Italy 1 Mexico 1 | | | | Norway 0 Rep. of Ireland 0 | | | |

| | P | W | D | L | F | A | Pts |
|---|---|---|---|---|---|---|---|
| Mexico | 3 | 1 | 1 | 1 | 3 | 3 | 4 |
| Italy | 3 | 1 | 1 | 1 | 2 | 2 | 4 |
| Rep. of Ireland | 3 | 1 | 1 | 1 | 2 | 2 | 4 |
| Norway | 3 | 1 | 1 | 1 | 1 | 1 | 4 |

### orld Cup facts

**Oldest player to have played in the finals**
42 years and 39 days, Roger Milla (Cameroon), v Russia, 1994

Attacking midfielder Yordan Letchkov, pictured seconds after heading the winning goal in Bulgaria's shock 2–1 victory over Germany in the quarter-finals. 'It was the finest day in the history of Bulgarian football,' declared Dimitar Penev, the Bulgarian manager. His team's victory earned them a semi-final against Italy, for whom Roberto Baggio was in magisterial form. Orchestrated by him, the 'azurri' played some of the best football of the tournament, deservedly eliminating the Bulgarians. Victory, however, came at a cost: an injury to Baggio that threatened to exclude him from the final.

## Group F

Belgium 1 Morocco 0
Belgium 1 Holland 0
Belgium 0 Saudi Arabia 1

Holland 2 Saudi Arabia 1
Saudi Arabia 2 Morocco 1
Morocco 1 Holland 2

|              | P | W | D | L | F | A | Pts |
|--------------|---|---|---|---|---|---|-----|
| Holland      | 3 | 2 | 0 | 1 | 4 | 3 | 6   |
| Saudi Arabia | 3 | 2 | 0 | 1 | 4 | 3 | 6   |
| Belgium      | 3 | 2 | 0 | 1 | 2 | 1 | 6   |
| Morocco      | 3 | 0 | 0 | 3 | 2 | 5 | 0   |

## Second round

Germany 3 Belgium 2
Holland 2 Rep. of Ireland 0
Italy 2 Nigeria 1 after extra time
Spain 3 Switzerland 0
Sweden 3 Saudi Arabia 1

Romania 3 Argentina 2
Brazil 1 USA 0
Mexico 1 Bulgaria 1 (Bulgaria won
on penalties)

## Quarter-finals

Italy 2 Spain 1
Bulgaria 2 Germany 1

Brazil 3 Holland 2
Sweden 2 Romania 2 (Sweden
won on penalties)

## Semi-finals

Italy 2 Bulgaria 1

Brazil 1 Sweden 0

## Third place

Sweden 4 Bulgaria 0

## Final

Brazil 0 Italy 0 (Brazil won on penalties)

◄1 In a show of unity the Romanian team line up for the quarter-final against Sweden, their hair dyed peroxide blonde. Like so many of the other games in the 1994 competition, it was watched by an impressively large crowd—81,715. The match offered a fascinating clash of styles. While the Swedes played muscular football that relied on a solid defence, the Romanians favoured a more expansive approach, most of their play flowing through the left foot of Georghe Hagi, their playmaker, once dubbed 'the Maradona of the Balkans'. At the end of extra time, the two teams were tied 2–2. Ultimately, Romania lost 5–4 on penalties, the decisive moment occurring when the veteran Swedish goalkeeper Thomas Ravelli saved Miodrag Belodedici's spot-kick.

During a game against USA on 22 June 1994, the Colombian defender Andrés Escobar deflected the ball into his own net. His team lost the game 2–1 and was eliminated from the competition at the first-round stage. When he returned home soon afterwards, Escobar was shot dead outside a bar in Medellín. The killer shot him twelve times. Each time he pulled the trigger, he shouted 'Goooooooooal!' Escobar's murder was widely believed to have been ordered by a gambling syndicate that had bet an enormous amount of money on Colombia qualifying for the second round. Next day a BBC pundit, commenting on another match, said that 'the Argentine defender wants shooting for a mistake like that.' The BBC issued an apology.

Prior to the second-round match between Nigeria and Italy in the 1994 World Cup finals, Samson Emeka Omeruah, President of the Nigerian Football Federation, declared that his team wasn't scared of the Italians. 'We're the champions of Africa: what are you?' he added. 'Italy is world famous for the mafia and Fiat, not for football.' Nigeria went on to lose the match 2–1 in extra time.

In the 1994 tournament the USA fielded a team that included the midfielder Bobby Convey, who was partially blind in his left eye.

Tension shows on the face of Italian playmaker, Roberto Baggio, as he prepares to take what turned out to be the crucial penalty in the shoot-out at the end of his country's 0–0 draw with Brazil in the final. Baggio—nicknamed 'the Divine Pony-tail'—fluffed his opportunity, handing victory to an uncharacteristically functional Brazilian team, epitomised by Dunga, the hard-working, hard-tackling captain. 'I missed because I tried a powerful shot,' Baggio admitted. 'I went against my own nature. I shot towards Tafferel's right-hand corner, but I was worn out. I made a bad run-up to the ball, with my body too far backwards. Out of it, there came a wretched shot—rubbish.' Few Italian fans could disagree. Somehow it was an appropriately anti-climactic end to a dreary final.

# 1998 *France*

Brazil 2 Scotland 1                    Morocco 2 Norway 2
Scotland 1 Norway 1                    Brazil 3 Morocco 0
Norway 2 Brazil 1                      Scotland 0 Morocco 3

|          | P | W | D | L | F | A | Pts |
|----------|---|---|---|---|---|---|-----|
| Brazil   | 3 | 2 | 0 | 1 | 6 | 3 | 6   |
| Norway   | 3 | 1 | 2 | 0 | 5 | 4 | 5   |
| Morocco  | 3 | 1 | 1 | 1 | 5 | 5 | 4   |
| Scotland | 3 | 0 | 1 | 2 | 2 | 6 | 1   |

## Group B

Italy 2 Chile 2                        Cameroon 1 Austria 1
Chile 1 Austria 1                      Italy 3 Cameroon 0
Italy 2 Austria 1                      Chile 1 Cameroon 1

|          | P | W | D | L | F | A | Pts |
|----------|---|---|---|---|---|---|-----|
| Italy    | 3 | 2 | 1 | 0 | 7 | 3 | 7   |
| Chile    | 3 | 0 | 3 | 0 | 4 | 4 | 3   |
| Austria  | 3 | 0 | 2 | 1 | 3 | 4 | 2   |
| Cameroon | 3 | 0 | 2 | 1 | 2 | 5 | 2   |

*trange but true*

Under American law, which banned commerce between the two countries, the match between the USA and Iran during the 1998 tournament was illegal.

Right-sided midfielder and renowned dead-ball specialist David Beckham scores with a spectacular swerving free kick to help England achieve a 2–0 opening-round victory over Colombia. In the next stage of the competition, however, Beckham and his team lost on penalties to Argentina. Beckham himself was controversially sent off after he aimed a petulant kick at Argentina's Diego Simeone. His dismissal was the crucial moment in a game of remarkable drama. Blamed for England's defeat, Beckham was the target of recurrent booing and abuse when he played club football for Manchester United the following season.

## Group C

Saudi Arabia 0 Denmark 1
South Africa 1 Denmark 1
France 2 Denmark 1

France 3 South Africa 0
France 4 Saudi Arabia 0
South Africa 2 Saudi Arabia 2

|  | P | W | D | L | F | A | Pts |
|---|---|---|---|---|---|---|---|
| France | 3 | 3 | 0 | 0 | 9 | 1 | 9 |
| Denmark | 3 | 1 | 1 | 1 | 3 | 3 | 4 |
| South Africa | 3 | 0 | 2 | 1 | 3 | 6 | 2 |
| Saudi Arabia | 3 | 0 | 1 | 2 | 7 | 7 | 1 |

## Group D

Paraguay 0 Bulgaria 0
Nigeria 1 Bulgaria 0
Nigeria 1 Paraguay 3

Spain 2 Nigeria 3
Spain 0 Paraguay 0
Spain 6 Bulgaria 1

|  | P | W | D | L | F | A | Pts |
|---|---|---|---|---|---|---|---|
| Nigeria | 3 | 2 | 0 | 1 | 5 | 5 | 6 |
| Paraguay | 3 | 1 | 2 | 0 | 3 | 1 | 5 |
| Spain | 3 | 1 | 1 | 1 | 8 | 4 | 4 |
| Bulgaria | 3 | 0 | 1 | 2 | 1 | 7 | 1 |

## Group E

South Korea 1 Mexico 3
Belgium 2 Mexico 2
Holland 2 Mexico 2

Holland 0 Belgium 0
Holland 5 South Korea 0
Belgium 1 South Korea 1

|  | P | W | D | L | F | A | Pts |
|---|---|---|---|---|---|---|---|
| Holland | 3 | 1 | 2 | 0 | 7 | 2 | 5 |
| Mexico | 3 | 1 | 2 | 0 | 7 | 5 | 5 |
| Belgium | 3 | 0 | 3 | 0 | 3 | 3 | 3 |
| South Korea | 3 | 0 | 1 | 2 | 2 | 9 | 1 |

## Group F

Yugoslavia 1 Iran 0
Germany 2 Yugoslavia 2
USA 0 Yugoslavia 1

Germany 2 USA 0
USA 1 Iran 2
Germany 2 Iran 0

|  | P | W | D | L | F | A | Pts |
|---|---|---|---|---|---|---|---|
| Germany | 3 | 2 | 1 | 0 | 6 | 2 | 7 |
| Yugoslavia | 3 | 2 | 1 | 0 | 4 | 2 | 7 |
| Iran | 3 | 1 | 0 | 2 | 2 | 4 | 3 |
| USA | 3 | 0 | 0 | 3 | 1 | 5 | 0 |

French goalkeeper Fabien Barthez, whose eccentric appearance was reflected in his performances on the pitch. Like the former Liverpool and Zimbabwe goalkeeper, Bruce Grobelaar, with whom he was often compared, he could produce moments of brilliance, but was also capable of costly moments of impetuousness. Despite his unpredictability and his country's lack of an international-class striker, France won the 1998 World Cup, inaugurating a period of Gallic dominance.

England 2 Tunisia 0
Colombia 1 Tunisia 0
Colombia 0 England 2

Romania 1 Colombia 0
Romania 2 England 1
Romania 1 Tunisia 1

|          | P | W | D | L | F | A | Pts |
|----------|---|---|---|---|---|---|-----|
| Romania  | 3 | 2 | 1 | 0 | 4 | 2 | 7   |
| England  | 3 | 2 | 0 | 1 | 5 | 2 | 6   |
| Colombia | 3 | 1 | 0 | 2 | 1 | 3 | 3   |
| Tunisia  | 3 | 0 | 1 | 2 | 1 | 4 | 1   |

## Group H

Argentina 1 Japan 0
Japan 0 Croatia 1
Argentina 1 Croatia 0

Jamaica 1 Croatia 3
Argentina 5 Jamaica 0
Japan 1 Jamaica 2

|           | P | W | D | L | F | A | Pts |
|-----------|---|---|---|---|---|---|-----|
| Argentina | 3 | 3 | 0 | 0 | 7 | 0 | 9   |
| Croatia   | 3 | 2 | 0 | 1 | 4 | 2 | 6   |
| Jamaica   | 3 | 1 | 0 | 2 | 3 | 9 | 3   |
| Japan     | 3 | 0 | 0 | 3 | 1 | 4 | 0   |

## Second round

Brazil 4 Chile 1
Holland 2 Yugoslavia 1
Italy 1 Norway 0
France 1 Paraguay 0 after extra time
Romania 0 Croatia 1

Nigeria 1 Denmark 4
Argentina 2 England 2 (Argentina won on penalties)
Germany 2 Mexico 1

## Quarter-finals

Brazil 3 Denmark 2
Italy 0 France 0 (France won on penalties)

Holland 2 Argentina 1
Germany 0 Croatia 3

## Semi-finals

Brazil 1 Holland 1 (Brazil won on penalties)

France 2 Croatia 1

## Third place

Holland 1 Croatia 2

## Final

Brazil 0 France 3

◄ Mexican goalkeeper Jorge Campos wearing one of his trademark shirts, designed by himself. He made up for his relative lack of height with conspicuous speed and agility. He was also distinguished by his habit of straying outside the penalty area. First-choice goalkeeper for Mexico in both the 1994 and 1998 World Cup finals, he went on to win 130 caps for his country. Away from the international stage, he played for numerous clubs in Mexico and had stints in American Major League Soccer for LA Galaxy and Chicago Fire.

# 2002 Japan/South Korea

## Group A

France 0 Senegal 1
Denmark 1 Senegal 1
Denmark 2 France 0

Uruguay 1 Denmark 2
France 0 Uruguay 0
Senegal 3 Uruguay 3

| | P | W | D | L | F | A | Pts |
|---|---|---|---|---|---|---|---|
| Denmark | 3 | 2 | 1 | 0 | 5 | 2 | 7 |
| Senegal | 3 | 1 | 2 | 0 | 5 | 4 | 5 |
| Uruguay | 3 | 0 | 2 | 1 | 4 | 5 | 2 |
| France | 3 | 0 | 1 | 2 | 0 | 3 | 1 |

## Group B

Paraguay 2 South Africa 2
Spain 3 Paraguay 1
South Africa 2 Spain 3

Spain 3 Slovenia 1
South Africa 1 Slovenia 0
Slovenia 1 Paraguay 3

| | P | W | D | L | F | A | Pts |
|---|---|---|---|---|---|---|---|
| Spain | 3 | 3 | 0 | 0 | 9 | 4 | 9 |
| Paraguay | 3 | 1 | 1 | 1 | 6 | 6 | 4 |
| South Africa | 3 | 1 | 1 | 1 | 5 | 5 | 4 |
| Slovenia | 3 | 0 | 0 | 3 | 2 | 7 | 0 |

◨ The unmistakable features of Italian referee Pierluigi Collina, who contracted a severe form of alopecia that resulted in the loss of all his facial hair. He began refereeing in 1977. By 1988 he was officiating in the Italian third division—Serie C1 and Serie C2. Within three seasons he had been promoted, allowing him to referee games in the top two divisions. His status as one of the world's best referees was confirmed when, in 1995, he was placed on FIFA's list of officials for international games. Here he is seen shortly before kick-off in the most important match in his career: the 2002 World Cup final between Brazil and Germany in Yokohama. Before the game, Oliver Kahn, the German goalkeeper, said, 'Collina is a world-class referee. There's no doubt about it. But he doesn't bring luck, does he?' Kahn had twice been on the losing team in matches refereed by Collina. Those matches were Bayern Munich's 2–1 defeat by Manchester United in the 1999 UEFA Champions' League final, and Germany's 5–1 defeat by England in the qualifying campaign for the 2002 World Cup finals.

## Group C

| | | | | | | | |
|---|---|---|---|---|---|---|---|
Brazil 2 Turkey 1 | | | | China 0 Costa Rica 2 | | | |
Brazil 4 China 0 | | | | Costa Rica 1 Turkey 1 | | | |
Costa Rica 2 Brazil 5 | | | | Turkey 3 China 0 | | | |

| | P | W | D | L | F | A | Pts |
|---|---|---|---|---|---|---|---|
| Brazil | 3 | 3 | 0 | 0 | 11 | 3 | 9 |
| Turkey | 3 | 1 | 1 | 1 | 5 | 3 | 4 |
| Costa Rica | 3 | 1 | 1 | 1 | 5 | 6 | 4 |
| China | 3 | 0 | 0 | 3 | 0 | 9 | 0 |

## Group D

South Korea 2 Poland 0     USA 3 Portugal 2
South Korea 1 USA 1     Portugal 4 Poland 0
Portugal 0 South Korea 1     Poland 3 USA 1

| | P | W | D | L | F | A | Pts |
|---|---|---|---|---|---|---|---|
| South Korea | 3 | 2 | 1 | 0 | 4 | 1 | 7 |
| USA | 3 | 1 | 1 | 1 | 5 | 6 | 4 |
| Portugal | 3 | 1 | 0 | 2 | 6 | 4 | 3 |
| Poland | 3 | 1 | 0 | 2 | 3 | 7 | 3 |

## Group E

Rep. of Ireland 1 Cameroon 1     Germany 8 Saudi Arabia 0
Germany 1 Rep. of Ireland 1     Cameroon 1 Saudi Arabia 0
Cameroon 0 Germany 2     Saudi Arabia 0 Rep. of Ireland 3

| | P | W | D | L | F | A | Pts |
|---|---|---|---|---|---|---|---|
| Germany | 3 | 2 | 1 | 0 | 11 | 1 | 7 |
| Rep. of Ireland | 3 | 1 | 2 | 0 | 5 | 2 | 5 |
| Cameroon | 3 | 1 | 1 | 1 | 2 | 3 | 4 |
| Saudi Arabia | 3 | 0 | 0 | 3 | 0 | 12 | 0 |

England captain David Beckham savours the applause triggered by what must, surely, be his greatest moment as an international footballer. In the final minute of a crucial World Cup qualifying game against Greece, England was awarded a controversial free kick on the edge of the penalty-box. At that stage Beckham's team, which needed a draw to ensure qualification, was trailing 2–1. As he lined up the kick, 60,000 fans inside Old Trafford knew this would be England's last chance in the game. A few seconds later, they watched him curl the ball into the top of the Greek net—a fitting end to a game in which Beckham had, through a combination of skill and athleticism, exerted an increasingly dominant influence, constantly moving across midfield. According to the ProZone statistics for the match, he ran 17km, still a record for an England player during an international game.

## Group F

| | | | | | | | |
|---|---|---|---|---|---|---|---|
| Argentina 1 Nigeria 0 | | | | England 1 Sweden 1 | | | |
| Sweden 2 Nigeria 1 | | | | Argentina 0 England 1 | | | |
| Sweden 1 Argentina 1 | | | | Nigeria 0 England 0 | | | |

| | P | W | D | L | F | A | Pts |
|---|---|---|---|---|---|---|---|
| Sweden | 3 | 1 | 2 | 0 | 4 | 3 | 5 |
| England | 3 | 1 | 2 | 0 | 2 | 1 | 5 |
| Argentina | 3 | 1 | 1 | 1 | 2 | 2 | 4 |
| Nigeria | 3 | 0 | 1 | 2 | 1 | 3 | 1 |

## Group G

| | | | | | | | |
|---|---|---|---|---|---|---|---|
| Croatia 0 Mexico 1 | | | | Italy 2 Ecuador 0 | | | |
| Italy 1 Croatia 2 | | | | Mexico 2 Ecuador 1 | | | |
| Mexico 1 Italy 1 | | | | Ecuador 1 Croatia 0 | | | |

| | P | W | D | L | F | A | Pts |
|---|---|---|---|---|---|---|---|
| Mexico | 3 | 2 | 1 | 0 | 4 | 2 | 7 |
| Italy | 3 | 1 | 1 | 1 | 4 | 3 | 4 |
| Croatia | 3 | 1 | 0 | 2 | 2 | 3 | 3 |
| Ecuador | 3 | 1 | 0 | 2 | 2 | 4 | 3 |

## Group H

| | | | | | | | |
|---|---|---|---|---|---|---|---|
| Japan 2 Belgium 2 | | | | Russia 2 Tunisia 0 | | | |
| Japan 1 Russia 0 | | | | Tunisia 1 Belgium 1 | | | |
| Tunisia 0 Japan 2 | | | | Belgium 3 Russia 2 | | | |

| | P | W | D | L | F | A | Pts |
|---|---|---|---|---|---|---|---|
| Japan | 3 | 2 | 1 | 0 | 5 | 2 | 7 |
| Belgium | 3 | 1 | 2 | 0 | 6 | 5 | 5 |
| Russia | 3 | 1 | 0 | 2 | 4 | 4 | 3 |
| Tunisia | 3 | 0 | 1 | 2 | 1 | 5 | 1 |

## strange but true

In the Oceania section of the qualifying rounds for the 2002 World Cup, Australia twice broke the record for the most emphatic victory in a competitive international game. First, they beat Tonga 22–0, and two days later met American Samoa, the lowest ranked of all FIFA's 203 members. The final score was a 31–0 rout, with Archie Thompson racking up 13 goals—a world record for a single player in an international match.

English supporters, seen here during the opening-round draw with Sweden, travelled in large numbers to the Far East. Not for the first time, the expense wasn't justified by their team's performance. Lurching through to the quarter-finals with all the grace of a Saturday-night drunk, England ended up being eliminated by the capable but far from unbeatable Brazilians.

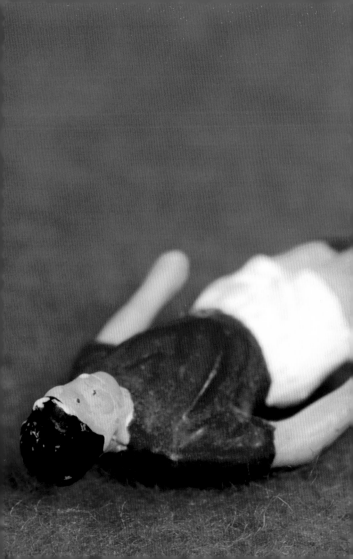

## Second round

Germany 1 Paraguay 0
Sweden 1 Senegal 2 after extra time
Mexico 0 USA 2
Brazil 2 Belgium 0
South Korea 2 Italy 1 after extra time

Denmark 0 England 3
Spain 1 Rep. of Ireland 1 (Spain won on penalties)
Japan 0 Turkey 1

## Quarter-finals

England 1 Brazil 2
Spain 0 South Korea 0 (South Korea won on penalties)

Germany 1 USA 0
Senegal 0 Turkey 1 after extra time

## Semi-finals

Germany 1 South Korea 0

Brazil 1 Turkey 0

## Third place

South Korea 2 Turkey 3

## Final

Brazil 2 Germany 0

### World Cup facts

**Only game in which two own-goals were scored**
USA v Portugal, 2002: the first came from Jorge Costa (Portugal) in the 29th minute, the second from Jeff Agoos (USA) in the 71st.

### World Cup facts

**Fastest goal in the finals**
11 seconds, Hakan Sukur (Turkey), v South Korea, 29 June 2002

### World Cup facts

**Youngest player in the qualifying tournament**
13 Years, 310 days, Souleymane Mamam (Togo), v Zambia, 2001

◢ Burly Italian striker Christian Vieri lies on his back in the goalmouth, having just missed an open goal. In one of the shocks of the tournament, co-hosts South Korea, under the inspirational management of Dutchman Guus Hiddink, defeated Italy 2–1. The result owed a great deal to a sequence of notoriously bad refereeing decisions. Hiddink, formerly in charge of the Dutch national team, went on to coach Australia in the 2006 World Cup finals and Russia in Euro 2008.

# 2006 *Germany*

Germany 4 Costa Rica 2          Poland 0 Ecuador 2
Germany 1 Poland 0             Ecuador 3 Costa Rica 0
Ecuador 0 Germany 3           Costa Rica 1 Poland 2

|            | P | W | D | L | F | A | Pts |
|------------|---|---|---|---|---|---|-----|
| Germany    | 3 | 3 | 0 | 0 | 8 | 2 | 9   |
| Ecuador    | 3 | 2 | 0 | 1 | 5 | 3 | 6   |
| Poland     | 3 | 1 | 0 | 2 | 2 | 4 | 3   |
| Costa Rica | 3 | 0 | 0 | 3 | 3 | 9 | 0   |

England 1 Paraguay 0              Trinidad & Tobago 0 Sweden 0
England 2 Trinidad & Tobago 0     Sweden 1 Paraguay 0
Sweden 2 England 2               Paraguay 2 Trinidad & Tobago 0

|                   | P | W | D | L | F | A | Pts |
|-------------------|---|---|---|---|---|---|-----|
| England           | 3 | 2 | 1 | 0 | 5 | 2 | 7   |
| Sweden            | 3 | 1 | 2 | 0 | 3 | 2 | 5   |
| Paraguay          | 3 | 1 | 0 | 2 | 2 | 2 | 3   |
| Trinidad & Tobago | 3 | 0 | 1 | 2 | 0 | 4 | 1   |

## trange but true

As a cruel practical joke, during the 2006 finals an Austrian artist filled two footballs with concrete, chained them to a lamppost and wrote 'Can you kick it?' on the pavement next to them. At least two fans who rose to the challenge found themselves in a Berlin hospital.

## trange but true

Some Dutch fans at the 2006 finals ended up watching in their underpants. Officials had made them take off their orange trousers because they carried the logo of Dutch brewer Bavaria—not the tournament's official beer sponsor.

In the wake of his spectacular Premier League debut for Everton, Wayne Rooney was the subject of a multi-million-pound transfer to Manchester United. Like the similarly squat, muscular and talented Paul Gascoigne sixteen years earlier, he used the World Cup to exhibit his prodigious skills.

## Group C

| | | | | | | | |
|---|---|---|---|---|---|---|---|
Argentina 2 Ivory Coast 1

Argentina 6 Serbia & Montenegro 0

Ivory Coast 3 Serbia & Montenegro 2

Serbia & Montenegro 0 Holland 1

Holland 2 Ivory Coast 1

Holland 0 Argentina 0

| | P | W | D | L | F | A | Pts |
|---|---|---|---|---|---|---|---|
| Argentina | 3 | 2 | 1 | 0 | 8 | 1 | 7 |
| Holland | 3 | 2 | 1 | 0 | 3 | 1 | 7 |
| Ivory Coast | 3 | 1 | 0 | 2 | 5 | 6 | 3 |
| Serbia & Montenegro | 3 | 0 | 0 | 3 | 2 | 10 | 0 |

## Group D

Mexico 3 Iran 1

Mexico 0 Angola 0

Portugal 2 Mexico 1

Angola 0 Portugal 1

Portugal 2 Iran 0

Iran 1 Angola 1

| | P | W | D | L | F | A | Pts |
|---|---|---|---|---|---|---|---|
| Portugal | 3 | 3 | 0 | 0 | 5 | 1 | 9 |
| Mexico | 3 | 1 | 1 | 1 | 4 | 3 | 4 |
| Angola | 3 | 0 | 2 | 1 | 1 | 2 | 2 |
| Iran | 3 | 0 | 1 | 2 | 2 | 6 | 1 |

## Group E

USA 0 Czech Republic 3

Czech Republic 0 Ghana 2

Czech Republic 0 Italy 2

Italy 2 Ghana 0

Italy 1 USA 1

Ghana 2 USA 1

| | P | W | D | L | F | A | Pts |
|---|---|---|---|---|---|---|---|
| Italy | 3 | 2 | 1 | 0 | 5 | 1 | 7 |
| Ghana | 3 | 2 | 0 | 1 | 4 | 3 | 6 |
| Czech Republic | 3 | 1 | 0 | 2 | 3 | 4 | 3 |
| USA | 3 | 0 | 1 | 2 | 2 | 6 | 1 |

## strange but true

After qualifying for the World Cup in 1950, India asked FIFA's permission to play in bare feet. The request was turned down, and India decided not to take part.

◄ Liverpool and England midfielder Steven Gerrard celebrates his last-minute goal against Trinidad & Tobago. His left-foot strike lent the scoreline a decisive impression not justified by the match, during which his team had struggled against the Carribean minnows. Though he made his first international appearance in 2000, Gerrard had to wait until 2006 before making his debut in the World Cup finals. Four years earlier he'd had to withdraw from England's World Cup squad due to a long-standing groin injury. In the 2006 tournament, he finished as England's top scorer—netting two goals—yet he missed one of the penalties during the quarter-final shoot-out defeat by Portugal.

## Group F

Australia 3 Japan 1
Croatia 0 Japan 0
Japan 1 Brazil 4

Brazil 1 Croatia 0
Brazil 2 Australia 0
Croatia 2 Australia 2

| | P | W | D | L | F | A | Pts |
|---|---|---|---|---|---|---|---|
| Brazil | 3 | 3 | 0 | 0 | 7 | 1 | 9 |
| Australia | 3 | 1 | 1 | 1 | 5 | 5 | 4 |
| Croatia | 3 | 0 | 2 | 1 | 2 | 3 | 2 |
| Japan | 3 | 0 | 1 | 2 | 2 | 7 | 1 |

## Group G

South Korea 2 Togo 1
France 1 South Korea 1
Togo 0 France 2

France 0 Switzerland 0
Togo 0 Switzerland 2
Switzerland 2 South Korea 0

| | P | W | D | L | F | A | Pts |
|---|---|---|---|---|---|---|---|
| Switzerland | 3 | 2 | 1 | 0 | 4 | 0 | 7 |
| France | 3 | 1 | 2 | 0 | 3 | 1 | 5 |
| South Korea | 3 | 1 | 1 | 1 | 3 | 4 | 4 |
| Togo | 3 | 0 | 0 | 3 | 1 | 6 | 0 |

## Group H

Spain 4 Ukraine 0
Saudi Arabia 0 Ukraine 4
Saudi Arabia 0 Spain 1

Tunisia 2 Saudi Arabia 2
Spain 3 Tunisia 1
Ukraine 1 Tunisia 0

| | P | W | D | L | F | A | Pts |
|---|---|---|---|---|---|---|---|
| Spain | 3 | 3 | 0 | 0 | 8 | 1 | 9 |
| Ukraine | 3 | 2 | 0 | 1 | 5 | 4 | 6 |
| Tunisia | 3 | 0 | 1 | 2 | 3 | 6 | 1 |
| Saudi Arabia | 3 | 0 | 1 | 2 | 2 | 7 | 1 |

## strange but true

Ready for the 2006 tournament, a giant brothel was constructed for visiting fans. Located only yards from the main stadium in Berlin, it had more than 100 rooms, plus a sauna and lap-dancing bar. A spokesman for the man who financed the project said, 'Football and sex go extremely well together.'

◁ The inconsistent Portuguese forward, Nuno Gomes, heads a consolation goal in his side's 3–1 defeat by Germany in the third-place match. Gomez was part of a group of players once dubbed 'the Golden Generation'. Those exceptionally gifted players included Luis Figo and Rui Costa, whose talents earned them lucrative contracts with top European club sides. For the majority of them, the 2006 World Cup finals represented their last chance to fulfil their promise on the international stage.

## Second round

Germany 2 Sweden 0
Argentina 2 Mexico 1 after extra time
Italy 1 Australia 0
Brazil 3 Ghana 0
Spain 1 France 3

England 1 Ecuador 0
Portugal 1 Holland 0
Switzerland 0 Ukraine 0 (Ukraine won on penalties)

## Quarter-finals

Germany 1 Argentina 1 (Germany won on penalties)
Brazil 0 France 1

Italy 3 Ukraine 0
England 0 Portugal 0 (Portugal won on penalties)

## Semi-finals

Germany 0 Italy 2 after extra time

Portugal 0 France 1

## Third place

Germany 3 Portugal 1

## Final

Italy 1 France 1 (Italy won on penalties)

orld Cup facts

**Most sendings-off in a single tournament**
28 2006

strange but true

For the 1986 World Cup finals FIFA banned players from swapping shirts, to spare viewers the sight of bare torsos.

French midfielder Zinedine Zidane, nicknamed 'Zizou', headbutts the Italian centre-half Marco Materazzi during the final. Zidane's sending off, which helped Italy to win a tight game, provided an ignominious conclusion to a great career. He made his league debut in 1988, playing for Cannes. His impressive performances eventually earned him a transfer to Bordeaux, where he was part of the team that finished runners-up in the 1995–96 UEFA Cup. By then, he'd gained his first cap for the French national team, coming on as a 63rd-minute substitute in a friendly against the Czech Republic, against whom he scored two goals. He would go on to win 108 caps, and be a part of the side that captured the 1998 World Cup and won Euro 2000. His club career, encompassing spells at Juventus and Real Madrid, was just as illustrious, the highlight being the 2002 UEFA Champions' League triumph with Real Madrid. He also won FIFA World Player of the Year on three occasions, an achievement only matched by the Brazilian striker Ronaldo.

# Acknowledgements

The authors would like to thank:

Peter Adolph

Julian Benson

Jeremy Day

Henri Delaunay

FIFA

Marc Glendening

Hasbro

John Inverdale

Ken Leeder

Jules Rimet

Dina Spector

Daryl Sznyter

Graham Taylor

and of course you the reader. You could make them really grateful by buying their other book…